# THE GOLDEN JET

# THE GOLDEN JET

## BOBBY HULL
## WITH BOB VERDI

**TRIUMPH**
BOOKS

Triumph Books and colophon are registered trademarks of
Random House, Inc.

Library of Congress Cataloging-in-Publication Data
Hull, Bobby, 1939-
 The Golden Jet / Bobby Hull with Bob Verdi.
    p. cm.
 ISBN 978-1-60078-405-7
1.  Hull, Bobby, 1939- 2.  Hockey players-Canada-Biography.  I. Verdi,
Bob. II. Title.
 GV848.5.H8A3 2010
 796.962092—dc22
 [B]
                                                      2010029283

This book is available in quantity at special discounts for your group or
organization. For further information, contact:

**Triumph Books**
542 South Dearborn Street
Suite 750
Chicago, Illinois 60605
(312) 939-3330
Fax (312) 663-3557
www.triumphbooks.com

Printed in U.S.A.
ISBN: 978-1-60078-405-7
Design by Wagner/Donovan Design
Photos courtesy of Bobby Hull and the Chicago Blackhawks unless otherwise
indicated

# THE GOLDEN JET
# CONTENTS

THIS IS 1943 when I was four years old. It was shortly after Christmas and I was dressed for a Canadian winter. On my hands are my father's old horse-hair-filled hockey gloves, and in my hands is a snow shovel. I could be on my way to the open-air rink to start shoveling snow to make a spot to skate. The rink was just across the field from our house, and I always walked there with my skates on. This photo was taken in the backyard of our modest home in Point Anne.

# CHAPTER ONE

# Bobby's Beginnings

ROBERT MARVIN HULL WAS BORN ON JANUARY 3, 1939, in Point Anne, Ontario, the fifth of 11 children. His father, Robert Sr., was a laborer for the Canada Cement Company and an imposing figure with a lot of energy and strength. It was said that Robert Sr. could lift up either end of a car; he also was a pretty fair hockey player.

Bobby Jr. didn't waste any time becoming acquainted with the sport that was indigenous to his town and country. When he was just a tyke, Bobby found himself in a pair of skates, laced up by sisters Barbara and Laura. Bobby gravitated toward an outdoor rink belonging to his dad's company, and the rest really is history.

Bobby was assigned the usual chores as time went on. "When I grew to maybe six or seven years old, I would get up at the crack of dawn," he recalled. "I would take care of the fire in the kitchen and get the water in the porridge pot on so Mom could prepare breakfast for all of us. Then I would pretty much disappear. I would head for that rink and spend the whole weekend there, sometimes just by myself, shooting the puck in the early morning and making enough noise that I likely woke up the rest of the neighborhood. I only came home for meals and often went right back to the rink after supper, where my sisters or father would have to bring me back home to go to bed. That was my routine every weekend."

Bobby built his strength by chopping down trees, walking four miles to and from school, or shoveling snow. He was muscular even as a youth, and with many hours under the tutelage of his father, Bobby learned skills such as stickhandling, passing, shooting, and protecting the puck while in his possession. As a parent, Bobby would jokingly tell his children that once in organized hockey he would play four games in four different leagues on a Saturday and collect at least 20 goals. It was obvious that he was a natural, particularly to Bob Wilson, a scout with the Blackhawks. Back in that era, it was commonplace for NHL teams to designate a special player as "property" and the Blackhawks gained the rights to Bobby, with family permission, at the age of 13.

Part of the process included leaving home, which Bobby did for a Junior B team in Hespeler, Ontario, about 170 miles away. "Dad worked at the same place forever," Bobby recalled. "So I left home at 14." Eventually, after playing Junior B for the Woodstock Warriors and winning the All-Ontario championship, Bobby joined the St. Catharines Teepees, the Blackhawks' Junior A farm team. Before long, Bobby was a star, but not one to forget the sacrifices made by his parents. "They put their lives on hold for me," said the man who became the greatest left wing in NHL annals. ∎

# JANUARY 3, 1939

## ROBERT MARVIN HULL IS BORN IN POINT ANNE, ONTARIO.

MY DAD IS THIRD FROM THE LEFT ON THE TOP ROW WITH THE CANADA CEMENT CLUB JUNIOR TEAM. It was a pretty good team, too, as you can see by the three pieces of hardware it won as Junior champions: the Leybourne, Burrows, and Plant No. 5 trophies. Dad was a left wing, and from everything I heard, not necessarily from him, he could really play. He could handle the puck and could splinter the boards around the rink with his shot, as I learned when he started teaching me. Dad was known as the "Blond Flash" when he played in Belleville, the town seven miles west of Point Anne.

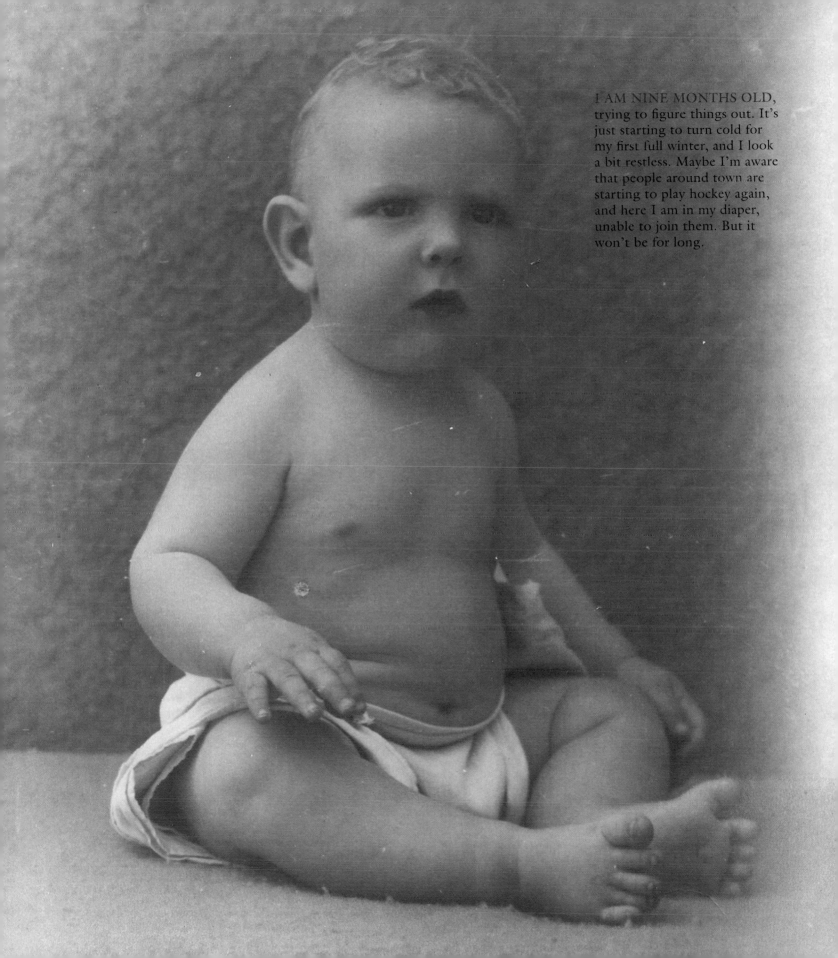

I AM NINE MONTHS OLD, trying to figure things out. It's just starting to turn cold for my first full winter, and I look a bit restless. Maybe I'm aware that people around town are starting to play hockey again, and here I am in my diaper, unable to join them. But it won't be for long.

LIKE I SAID, IT DIDN'T TAKE LONG. This is me at age six on the Bay of Quinte, where I probably spent as much time as I did in bed. I am too young to be playing on a team yet, but I do recall that I was perfectly happy being out there alone or with my sisters, just skating hour after hour. I was one of the few kids who shoveled snow to clear space to play. Two clumps of snow at either end would become the goals. If I had a dollar for every time I shoveled snow off that old outdoor rink on the Bay of Quinte, I would have been a rich kid. But I was usually first to arrive, and was only too happy to serve.

THIS IS DURING THE SUMMER, so we had to make our fun without ice. I am sitting on my father's broad shoulders. Sisters Jackie, left, and Maxine, right, are posing. Dad was a hard worker, but he always made time for the family. This photo was taken at Frank and Ellie Howard's farm near Roslyn, Ontario.

FIRST GRADE IN POINT ANNE. I am third from the left on the bottom row. I wasn't much of a student, but my parents taught me life's lessons, and I learned a lot on my own. I can speak some French, a few words of Russian, and some Slovak taught to me by my good friend and teammate, Stan Mikita, and I didn't go to school for that. Our teacher, Dina Baxter, was a tough one. Doesn't she look the part?

AT AGE 11, I was a second-year bantam in the Belleville minor league. Our team was the Bruins. My dad is at the upper right, and I am lower left (circled). Mom came to the games but stayed far away from Dad, who thought he was the coach and was very much into it. Our coach was Dan Cowley, whose brother Bill was a great player for the Boston Bruins in the 1930s. Lloyd "Red" Doran, far left in the back row, played some pro hockey, while Orlaf Boyler Lloyd was our manager.

THIS IS THE MEN'S SENIOR LEAGUE I PLAYED IN. I was 12 or 13, and most of the other guys were older, as you can see. Dad is in a suit on the left, I am second from the lower right. In those days, the slogan in Canada was, "Take your boy to the rink, don't send him." That still works for me.

BY THE AGE OF **12** BOBBY WAS ALREADY COMPETING IN A MEN'S SENIOR LEAGUE.

I'VE SCORED TWO GOALS IN THE MEN'S SENIOR LEAGUE, and I'm proud of it. Dad is cracking a smile. Dad was impatient with me on occasion, but always in a good way. He was a great mentor. He would skate with me all the time and taught me how to keep the puck on my stick as I skated. "Keep your head up," he would say, "and if your blade is angled properly, the puck will feel right on it." Sticks weren't as expensive then. If you look closely, you'll see the price of one right below Dad's hands: one dollar. That won't buy a stick now.

I LOVED TO PLAY BASEBALL, TOO. On the far right, seated, I played with Robb's Royals when I was 12. I played all over. I pitched, I was an outfielder, and I could hit. I was always busy with sports.

THIS IS A YEAR LATER, on another team in Belleville, Robb's Rockets. I am on the left, second row, on my knees. I'm 13 here, and if you compare this with the picture on the left, I'd grown a fair bit in one year. Many of my good friends from hockey also played ball together.

FOOTBALL WAS ANOTHER GAME I REALLY ENJOYED. This is the St. Catharines High School Institute team. I am No. 15, fourth from the lower left, a fullback and linebacker. No platoons in those days. I was recruited by Colorado State, and scouts from the Hamilton Tiger Cats said I likely could have played defense for them.

BEFORE ST. CATHARINES AND WOODSTOCK, there was my move to the Hespeler Hawks of the Ontario Junior B league. I was 14, I had to leave home, and I lived in a rooming house in Preston while playing hockey and going to high school. Remember, I belonged to the Blackhawks by then, I was theirs until they decided they didn't want me. From left are Harry Chalk, Dick Beitz, yours truly, and Reno Alberton, wearing the "A." Carl Hatt is eating the orange. Carl followed me to Woodstock where he looked after me as my left winger. You had to grow up early leaving home at that age, but it was my decision. Hockey was my passion.

WOODSTOCK WAS NEXT, and at 15 I was part of our All-Ontario Junior B champions. I am the first player from the left in the middle row. Matt Ravlich, a future teammate of mine in Chicago, is the fourth player from the right, same row. A great year in hockey—and school, too. I made the honors list! Carl Hatt is the sixth player from the left in that middle row, while right winger "Winkey" Ragers is to my left.

HESPELER HAWKS, 1953–54. Gary Venna is on the left and Reno Alberton is on the right. I just arrived, so Venna beat me to the No. 9 jersey. Bill Hastings was my first coach there. I always felt if the object is to win and if I can score, why pass the puck? Bill helped broaden my horizons.

ST. CATHARINES TEE-PEES, 1956–57. I am third from the right in the front row. Rudy Pilous is the coach. To his right in the back row are Stan Mikita and Chico Maki. John McKenzie is on the far right, front row. Wayne Hillman is in the middle row, fourth from the right. All future NHLers. Not a bad team, eh? On Hillman's left are Reno Rembaza and captain Ed Hoekstra, who also played some pro hockey.

THIS COULD BE MY FIRST OFFICIAL PRESS PHOTOGRAPH
AS A MEMBER OF THE ST. CATHARINES TEEPEES, when I was
16. I started out as a center, and you'll notice there's not much curve
to my stick blade. That would change. St. Catharines is a nice little
city in southwestern Ontario, about 30 miles from Buffalo. I didn't
know it at the time, but years before I went there, the Blackhawks
scouted me. Bob Wilson, a Blackhawks scout, came to Belleville when
I was 12, and soon I was on their negotiation list. He later said he
knew, even when I was a kid, that I would make it to the NHL.

STAN MIKITA IS ON THE LEFT AND PAT ADAIR IS IN THE MIDDLE ON THE TEEPEES. Nowadays, there are several ways for a young man to advance to the NHL. But back then, the league featured almost all players born in Canada, and almost all had to do what I did—leave home to chase the dream. If I had had a scholarship offer from a university, which is common now, I might have taken that road. But I never had any regrets or pressure from my parents. We lived well and never wanted for anything. Dad said I was so cheap with money I earned on the side, I wouldn't have paid a dime to see Niagara Falls flow backward. Dad and Mom wore out three cars to see me play in Hespeler, Woodstock, and St. Catharines. And whenever I went home, they were there with open arms.

STAN AND I ARE CELEBRATING SOMETHING. He was No. 9 and I was No. 8, by the way. Also, he was my right wing. I was a center. They hadn't figured out yet that Stan was too smart to be a right wing, and I was too dumb to be a center.

# 8 THE JERSEY NUMBER BOBBY WORE AS A MEMBER OF THE ST. CATHARINES TEEPEES.

THIS IS FROM THE 1961–62 SEASON, a year when I made history of sorts by becoming just the third player in history to score 50 goals in one season. Maurice "Rocket" Richard of the Montreal Canadiens had 50 during the 1944–45 season when they only played 50 games, which was pretty amazing. Bernie "Boom Boom" Geoffrion, also of the Canadiens, had 50 in 1960–61 with the expanded schedule of 70 games. I had 50 goals and 34 assists this season to win the scoring title over Andy Bathgate of the New York Rangers, who also had 84 points but just 28 goals. We each received the $1,000 first prize.

# CHAPTER TWO

# The Golden Jet Takes Flight

**P**ROSPECTS ARE PLENTIFUL IN SPORTS. Youngsters who "can't miss" making it to the big time, the professional level, are everywhere. Naturally, most of them are not ready, willing, or able to make the grade. But Robert Marvin Hull was destined for the NHL. He had the genetic ability, as well as the passion. Whenever his confidence lapsed, which wasn't often, Hull was buoyed by a supporting cast led by his father and mother. When Bobby joined the St. Catharines Teepees of the Ontario Hockey Association—Junior A, one step from the pros—it was reasonable to assume he would log a few seasons there honing his skills. In his first full year, 1955–56, Hull registered 11 goals and seven assists in 48 games. The coach there was Rudy Pilous, who leaned on his prodigy to pass the puck more. "You're a center," Pilous intoned. "Your main job is not to carry the puck." Pilous switched Hull to left wing, but that created stress in their relationship. Hull rebelled briefly and left for home, but returned at the behest of his parents. If Bobby, at age 18, wasn't sure about his future, his mother was. "You can make the team," she said, meaning the Blackhawks. Bobby scored 33 goals, along with 28 assists, for St. Catharines in 1956–57, thus earning him an invitation to try out for the Blackhawks when they were to train there the next autumn.

Come September, Bobby was doing his thing in St. Catharines—school, hockey, football—when he got the call. The Blackhawks had an exhibition game that night against the New York Rangers and he was listed on the Chicago roster. He had a full meal at the home of Orv and Eve Christie—roast beef, mashed potatoes, gravy, vegetables—then went out an hour later and clicked for a couple goals against Lorne "Gump" Worsley, a veteran netminder for the Rangers. "I was lucky," said Hull. But Tommy Ivan, the Blackhawks' general manager, knew otherwise. After a bit of tough bargaining, Bobby became the second-youngest player in the NHL. "I got lucky again," he recalled. "In my seventh game with Chicago, we were playing the Boston Bruins. Don Simmons was their goalie. Somebody let me have it pretty good. I went down, right on top of the puck. Basically, I just slid into the cage along with the puck. Not very impressive, but it was a start. My first NHL goal."

Hull wound up with 13 goals in 1957–58, and his coach was none other than Pilous, who also had been promoted from St. Catharines to Chicago. Hull finished second to Frank Mahovlich in voting for the Calder Memorial Trophy as best rookie. Mahovlich had 20 goals for Toronto. But in time, the Golden Jet would gather many more goals and trophies. ■

# BOBBY MADE HIS NHL DEBUT AT THE AGE OF 18.

I AM A ROOKIE TRY-ING TO MAKE MY WAY THROUGH TRAFFIC IN ANOTHER FABULOUS BUILDING, the Montreal Forum. I have broken my stick while tangling with Jean Beliveau, one of the most elegant players, on and off the ice, in any era. He could do it all, and as time went on during my career, the Blackhawks and Canadiens had some tremen-dous battles. Jean-Guy Talbot is in the background. Another wardrobe note: when I came up, the numbers were above the tomahawk on the sleeve. Later, that was reversed.

MY THIRD CAREER GOAL, November 10, 1957, against the Toronto Maple Leafs and goalie Ed Chadwick at the Stadium. Eric Nesterenko and Hec Lalonde assisted.

I AM OUTNUMBERED BY THE BOSTON BRUINS BEHIND THEIR NET. On the left, wearing the "A," is Allan Stanley, a defenseman who played a long time in the NHL, including a brief tour with the Blackhawks. Don Simmons is the goalie—without a mask, you'll notice. That's the way it was back in the day. Larry Hillman is trying to keep me away from the puck. I scored my first NHL goal against the Bruins in 1957. They weren't a powerhouse, and we weren't either in my rookie year. But in the Original Six, you played each other often, and every game felt like a big one.

WITH MY STRAIGHT BLADE, I am practicing and posing at Rainbo Arena, our practice rink. As I got into the NHL routine, I realized all those hours I spent skating as a kid were worthwhile. The more natural you feel on skates, the more you can think about other parts of the game. Skating should be like walking. You don't think about taking each step, you just do it.

# 13

## THE NUMBER OF GOALS BOBBY SCORED AS A ROOKIE IN 1957–58.

IN JANUARY OF 1958, Tommy Ivan gave up the dual responsibilities of general manager/coach and named a new coach, Rudy Pilous, whom I played under as a junior in St. Catharines. He wasn't well known within NHL circles, but Ivan thought he would be a good fit in Chicago. Pilous is on the left with Pierre Pilote (wearing No. 21, a number Stan Mikita would make famous). To my left are Ian Cushenan and another defenseman, Elmer "Moose" Vasko, who turned out to be a vital part of the Blackhawks as we built a strong team.

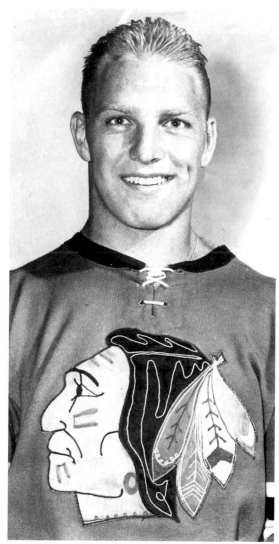

COACH PILOUS IS SHARING HIS WISDOM WITH YOURS TRULY; Stan Mikita, who joined the Blackhawks briefly from St. Catharines in 1958–59 before beginning his great career the next season; and Eric Nesterenko, who came to Chicago from the Toronto Maple Leafs and played forever, too. Eric was a scholar. He went to college while playing in the NHL.

IF IT LOOKS AS THOUGH I AM HAPPY TO BE A MEMBER OF THE BLACK-HAWKS, it's because I was. Chicago was a whole new world for me. A big city with a lot of people. But they were warm and friendly to us players, and they loved their hockey.

EARLY IN THE 1958–59 SEASON, ERIC NESTERENKO (LEFT) AND RON MURPHY (RIGHT) were among my line-mates. In later years, my brother Dennis wore No. 10.

EARLY IN THE 1958–59 SEASON, my second with the Blackhawks, we started to feel better about our chances, and we were onto something. The franchise had really struggled. Since 1946, the Blackhawks had made the playoffs once. But for the second time in 13 years, we qualified by finishing third. Pilote and Vasko, from the left, were stalwarts on defense, and Ed Litzenberger (middle) led us in scoring with 33 goals. To my left is No. 11 Lorne Ferguson. I had 18 goals in 70 games. Montreal knocked us out of the playoffs in six games in the first round.

I AM AT REST AGAINST THE NET, probably because Coach Pilous was looking in another direction. It was common then, and still is, for teams to practice
not only on off-days but on the morning of game days. Rudy Pilous was the guy
who implemented those game-day skates, much to my chagrin. If you look closely,
you'll see chicken wire above the boards. That's the way it was before Plexiglas.

I NEVER PAID MUCH ATTENTION TO STATISTICS. I knew that I was 5'10" and that I weighed 195 or so pounds, but I left it to others to talk about the "facts" that I could skate at speeds up to 30 miles per hour and that I could shoot the puck 120 miles per hour. I do know that being able to stop and start on skates is important. The flow of play in hockey is forever changing, and if you can't stop right away, if you glide around in a circular pattern, you'll wind up behind the action. I'm stopping here with a snow shower for proof.

ON DECEMBER 27, 1959, I had my third hat trick of the month, and second against Harry Lumley of the Boston Bruins, a Hall of Fame goalie. Our coach, Rudy Pilous, helps me enjoy the moment in the locker room.

MY 55TH CAREER GOAL ON JANUARY 2, 1960, in Maple Leaf Gardens. You can see the puck in the net, just below my left knee, while goalie Johnny Bower has lost the grip on his stick. Tim Horton, a tough and talented defenseman, is looking on while Murray Balfour is cheering me on from the ice and Bill Hay is excited behind the cage. It was always special playing in those old buildings of the Original Six, and Maple Leaf Gardens certainly was one of them. The fans there really knew their hockey.

I AM OFFICIALLY AN ADULT HERE as I play against the Toronto Maple Leafs on January 3, 1960, my 21st birthday. Gerry Ehman and I both want the puck, and our faces show the strain of a typical Original Six matchup, when we played the other five teams 14 times during the regular season.

HERE IS MY DAD PRACTICING WHAT HE PREACHED about protecting the puck while skating. He harped on that move with me, and it was a valuable lesson. It's tough to score without the biscuit.

ONE TROPHY THAT MIGHT NOT SHOW UP on my official NHL resume, but an honor I always will cherish, is the Most Valuable Player Award from the Blackhawk Standbys, the league's oldest team fan club. The Standbys sat all over at the Stadium, where they hung their banner, and every season a bunch of them traveled to some of our road games, either by bus or plane. They also had an annual banquet that all players attended. During the 2009–10 season, management brought the Standbys into the organization as the Blackhawks' official fan club, another good move by the brass.

I WON THREE ART ROSS TROPHIES DURING MY CAREER. This was the first, after I recorded 39 goals and 42 assists during the 1959–60 season. I had scored 13 and 18 goals, respectively, in my first two seasons with the Blackhawks, so I suppose you could say that this third season is when I really kicked it up a level or two. Bill Hay and Murray Balfour were my customary linemates. We made the playoffs, and I just beat out Bronco Horvath of the Bruins for the Ross. He also had 39 goals, tying for the league lead, but had one fewer assist (41) than I did.

I HAVE THE LOOK OF A HUNGRY LEFT WINGER in the quest for a rebound, sometime during the 1959–60 season. You'll note that our sweaters during that period of time featured the tie-down at the top. One of the great uniforms in sports, then and now.

ALL DRESSED UP IN OUR GEAR: from left are Pierre Pilote, Murray Balfour, yours truly, Bill Hay, and Jack Evans.

YOU CAN TELL THIS IS FROM A DIFFERENT ERA. Look at how those kids got dressed up for a trip to the Stadium, where they huddle with our captain, Ed Litzenberger, and yours truly along the boards of that great old building. Kids don't wear jackets and ties anymore, do they? Especially bow ties. This was our big year, before we won the Stanley Cup by surprising the Canadiens and then whipping Detroit in the finals. The next season, Litzenberger was gone to the Red Wings, then eventually to the Toronto Maple Leafs.

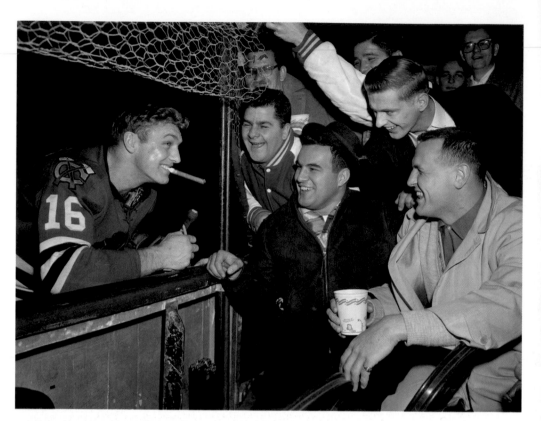

TRAINING CAMP IN ST. CATHARINES, ONTARIO, wasn't all work. I am about to have a cigar with some friends. I never smoked cigarettes, but I have enjoyed the occasional stogie.

I AM FIGHTING FOR POSSESSION OF THE PUCK with Doug Mohns of the Boston Bruins while my teammate Pierre Pilote is in the background along with Johnny Bucyk of the Bruins. Mohns played 11 seasons with the Bruins and was a left wing as well as a defenseman. Little did I know that he would become a teammate in Chicago. He probably didn't plan on it either. But in 1964, the Blackhawks acquired him in exchange for Reg Fleming and Ab McDonald, two veterans who had helped us win the 1961 Cup.

# BOBBY SCORED **62** CAREER PLAYOFF GOALS AS A MEMBER OF THE BLACKHAWKS.

I TAKE A TUMBLE WITH HENRI RICHARD (16) and his brother Maurice "Rocket" Richard surrounding me. Pierre Pilote is in front of goalie Glenn Hall, flanked by Montreal's Dickie Moore. The Rocket was one of the great clutch scorers ever, mean and determined. I liked him a lot. He would always come over and say hello. He also told me, "Bobby, don't get fat or you won't be able to play anymore." Scotty Bowman once said there were three players who could lift fans out of their seats: Howie Morenz, the Rocket, and yours truly. I have always considered that a great compliment.

I AM SHOOTING AGAINST THE CANADIENS during a regular-season game the year we won the Cup. We finished third in the league with 75 points, and the Canadiens wound up in first place with 92 points. But in the playoffs, anything can happen—and did.

I AM TOLD THIS IS A FAIRLY FAMOUS PICTURE OF ME BAILING HAY on my Ontario farm during the summer of 1961. It ran in *Time* magazine. Like I said, I never lifted weights. I didn't have to. That hay was heavy.

ANOTHER MOMENT FROM OUR STANLEY CUP YEAR. We are in Toronto, ganging up on Johnny Bower, the great Maple Leafs goalie, who has his eyes closed. Larry Hillman is the defenseman, and my teammate on the rush is Tod Sloan.

EARLY IN MY CAREER I WAS FULL OF HISS AND
VINEGAR, as you can see here as I wind up and come
around the net.

THE MONTREAL CANADIENS WERE SHOOTING FOR A RECORD SIXTH STRAIGHT STANLEY CUP WHEN WE UPSET THEM IN THE FIRST ROUND OF THE 1961 PLAY-OFFS. Gilles Trembley is on the left, and I'm trying to defend him in front of our great goalie, Glenn Hall. My teammate Murray Balfour and Montreal's Jean Beliveau are to Hall's right.

ON APRIL 4, 1961, we eliminated the Canadiens 4–2 in the semifinals after Hall registered consecutive shutouts in Games 5 and 6. We clinched with a 3–0 victory at the Stadium, where I celebrated with Bill Hay (left) and Eric Nesterenko.

AFTER WE BEAT MONTREAL, we made note of the huge stakes awaiting a Cup winner: $54,000 to be divided among all of us. That doesn't sound like a lot of money these days, but it was a nice incentive then.

GOALIE GLENN HALL AND I CELEBRATE OUR VICTORY AGAINST MONTREAL. Getting Hall from the Detroit Red Wings was one of the great trades in Blackhawks history.

THIS WAS FROM GAME 6 of the 1961 Stanley Cup Finals at the Olympia in Detroit.

A BIG GOAL FOR US. It might not look like much, but this was the eventual winner during Game 6 of the 1961 Stanley Cup Finals at the Detroit Olympia. I never got a shot off, but I did pile into Hank Bassen, the Red Wings' goalie. While Bassen lay there, Ab McDonald (14) swooped in to score. We went ahead 2–1 and never looked back, winning 5–1. Stan Mikita (21) was in on the play for us, as usual. Detroit's defenseman, No. 3, is Marcel Pronovost. Our other hero was Glenn Hall, whom we lifted on our shoulders at game's end.

# 23 YEARS BETWEEN STANLEY CUP CHAMPIONSHIPS FOR THE BLACKHAWKS (1937–38, 1960–61).

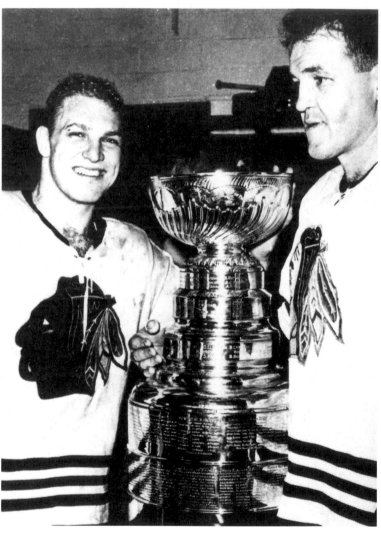

WHEN IT WAS OVER IN 1961, I was congratulated on our Cup victory at Detroit by the great Gordie Howe. That's one of the unique traditions in sports: after every NHL playoff series, no matter what went before, teams line up on the ice to shake hands.

ON APRIL 16, 1961, we culminated a long, tough climb by clinching the Stanley Cup in Detroit's Olympia, where we beat the Red Wings 5–1 to win the best-of-seven series 4–2. It was the first Stanley Cup for the Blackhawks since 1938, and it had to feel great to Chicago fans who suffered through a tough decade in the 1950s. Jack Evans, whose nickname was "Tex," joins me in the locker room. He began his career with the New York Rangers, then came to Chicago and was a stalwart on defense, a veteran who took no guff from anybody.

HERE I AM WITH THE 1961 STANLEY CUP after we returned to Chicago, where we all had a crack posing with it at the Stadium. On the night we clinched in Detroit, there was a huge snowstorm. That doesn't happen anymore, because the finals end in the middle of June, not the middle of April. Anyway, we couldn't fly back home, so we had a little party, one of a series, at a hotel in Detroit. Didn't matter. We could have won the Cup on the moon. For a kid growing up on skates, watching *Hockey Night in Canada* every Saturday night, winning the Stanley Cup was a dream fulfilled.

WHEN IT WAS ALL OVER, we got dressed up to take a look at the Stanley Cup, which bears the names of players on winning teams. It's a tremendous honor. I am looking things over with Reggie Fleming and Pierre Pilote, who appears to have a beverage in hand.

WE ARE CELEBRATING OUR 1961 STANLEY CUP VICTORY at City Hall in Chicago with the mayor, Richard J. Daley, who is at the left just under the flagpole. To his left are Arthur Wirtz, captain Ed Litzenberger, and James Norris. Wirtz and Norris owned the Blackhawks at the time. General manager Tommy Ivan is to Norris' left, and I'm in the light coat to Ivan's left. We had a nice celebration in Chicago, but it was nothing like the estimated 2 million people who attended the parade for the 2010 Stanley Cup champion Blackhawks.

THIS IS FROM DECEMBER OF 1961, the year we won the Cup. Must have been early in the game because my hair is perfectly combed.

# 16, 7, 9

## THE JERSEY NUMBERS BOBBY WORE DURING HIS NHL CAREER.

CHRISTMAS NIGHT, 1961. Yes, back in those days, we played on Christmas. They don't allow that anymore. I am wearing No. 7 now. When we won the Cup in the spring of 1961, I was wearing No. 16, as I had since I was a rookie. But the next season, I was slumping. This goal was only my 13th. So Walter "Gunzo" Humeniuk, our trainer and equipment expert, switched me to No. 7 and I went on a binge, winding up with 50 goals for the first time. Also, at a house I was renting in Maywood, I put a piece of plywood beneath the mattress. All of a sudden, I slept better and had more energy for the second half of the season. But I assured Gunzo it was the new number. I scored 37 goals in 35 games that year to reach 50 for the first time.

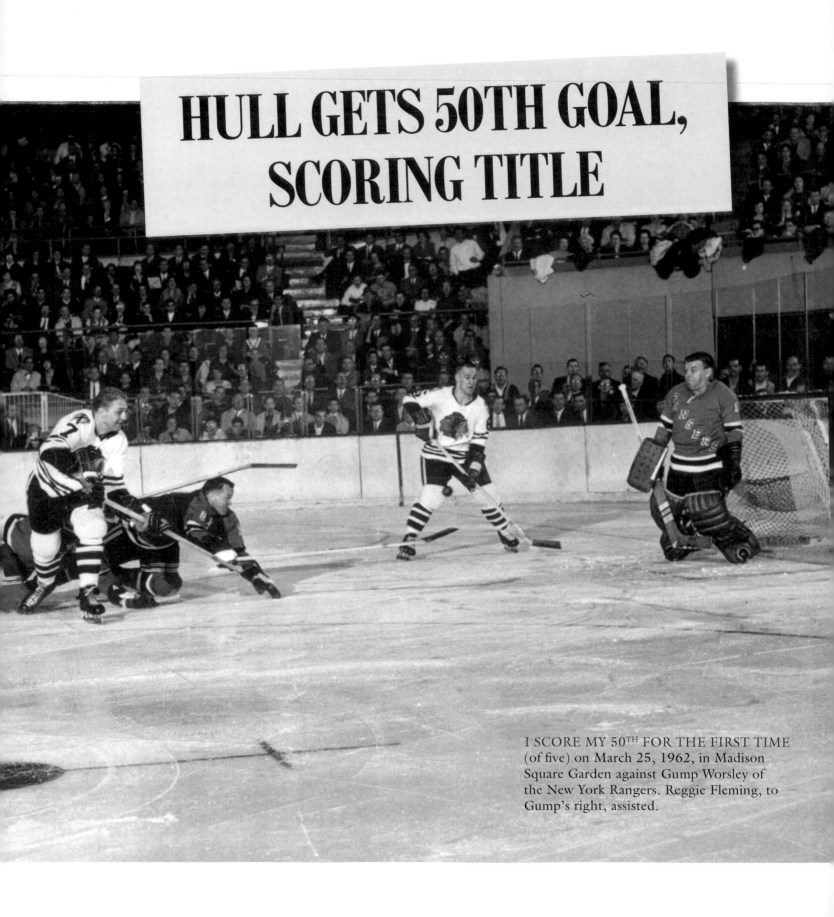

# HULL GETS 50TH GOAL, SCORING TITLE

I SCORE MY 50TH FOR THE FIRST TIME (of five) on March 25, 1962, in Madison Square Garden against Gump Worsley of the New York Rangers. Reggie Fleming, to Gump's right, assisted.

IN GAME 6 OF THE 1962 STANLEY CUP FINALS, I scored against goalie Johnny Bower of the Toronto Maple Leafs. The puck is in the back of the net; Bobby Baun, a rough and tough defenseman, is on my back. Murray Balfour (8) is on my left. We took a 1–0 lead in the Stadium on the goal, but the Maple Leafs rallied to score twice and win 2–1 to take the series. Bower was a key figure on a veteran Toronto team run by Punch Imlach, who brought the 33-year-old goalie up from the minor leagues when Bower thought he was done in the NHL.

WHO SAID ALL-STAR GAMES DON'T MEAN ANYTHING? In the 1963 game at Toronto, I am fighting with Tim Horton of the defending Stanley Cup champion Maple Leafs.

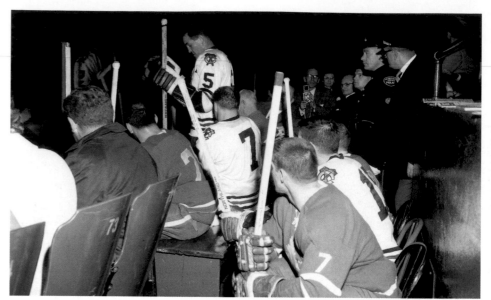

I AM NO. 7 IN CROWDED QUARTERS. Back in the day, players from both sides were sentenced to the same penalty box. It was not the ideal situation. Jack Evans is No. 5.

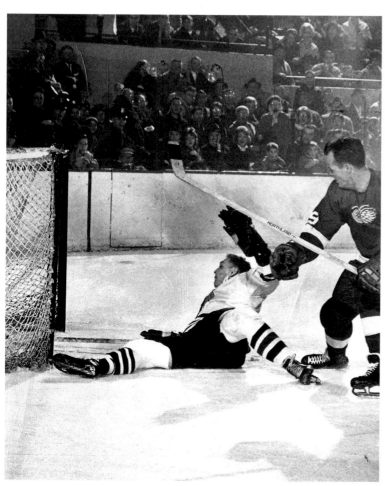

GORDIE HOWE TRIPS ME, but it was too late. I scored my 167th career goal on January 26, 1963, against goalie Hank Bassen, wherever he is.

ON FEBRUARY 10, 1963, I collected my 175th career goal against the New York Rangers, whose goalie Gump Worsley is down as the puck (arrow) enters the net. Murray Balfour, who assisted, is on the left with Rangers defenseman Larry Cahan (5). Don McKenney (11) was too late to help.

YOU CAN SEE THE PUCK BULGING IN THE BACK OF THE NET against Toronto's Don Simmons on my 172nd goal on February 3, 1963. Stan Mikita and Bill Hay assisted at the Stadium.

IN THE 1963 PLAYOFFS, Bruce MacGregor slashed me across the face in Game 2, fracturing my nose and giving me a black eye. We won the first two games, I sat out Game 3, and unfortunately we wound up losing four in a row to get eliminated.

DID SOMEONE SAY I DIDN'T PLAY BOTH ENDS OF THE ICE? Here I am helping to defend against the Detroit Red Wings. Our goalie is the one and only Glenn Hall.

GAME 1 OF THE STANLEY CUP SEMIFINALS against the Detroit Red Wings on March 26, 1963, at the Stadium. I score against goalie Hank Bassen with four of his teammates around me: Val Fonteyne (19), Norm Ullman, Bill Gadsby (4), and Doug Barkley (5). That's Murray Balfour (8) behind the net. We started off well in the series, winning this game 5–4 and the next one 5–2, both at home, as we scored four goals on power plays, including two on the penalty against Bruce MacGregor for the aforementioned slash on me.

TRAINING CAMP IN 1963 WITH MY NEW
NO. 9. My brother Dennis said I could shoot
the puck so hard, it could go through a car wash
without getting wet. Dennis also could fire it, but
as he said, his problem was hitting the car wash.

# CHAPTER THREE

# A Living Legend

WHEN EVALUATING THE CAREER OF BOBBY HULL, one feels strongly in two ways. Without question, the sheer magnitude of his statistics from bygone seasons solidify his place in hockey history. At 18, he debuted in a league of the Original Six—only a half-dozen franchises throughout North America. Today, there are 30. The Golden Jet, now in his seventies, is revered as the greatest left wing ever to lace up skates. He was a first-team All-Star in 10 of his 15 seasons with the Blackhawks. He won the Art Ross Trophy three times as the league's most prolific scorer, and in consecutive years, 1965 and 1966, earned the Hart Memorial Trophy awarded to the "player adjudged most valuable to his team." In 1965, he also received the Lady Byng Memorial Trophy presented to the individual who exhibits the best type of sportsmanship and gentlemanly conduct combined with a high standard of playing ability. He helped the Blackhawks win the Stanley Cup in 1961, he made the cover of *Time* magazine, and, of course, he was inducted into the Hockey Hall of Fame in 1983. Upon retirement, Hull was the second-most-prolific goal scorer in NHL annals and he ranked ninth in total points.

But here is the other dimension: space does not permit the litany of Hull's accomplishments as a goodwill ambassador for his team and his sport. The Golden Jet's creed was that fans deserved to be "entertained royally" with each and every one of his shifts on ice. However, Hull believed that his obligations did not end there. Part of his legend extends to the lobby of Chicago Stadium where, without fail, Hull signed autographs and posed for pictures night after night. He did not do so on the run, either. He stood until everybody was satisfied. Hull was no different on the road. In Canada, where hockey is part of the national fabric, he could not walk to dinner without attracting a crowd. Teammates will tell you of the ritual: they would board the bus after a game, only to wait until Hull completed his rounds, engaging fans who knew where players would exit and were eager to connect with the Golden Jet. They also knew he would not disappoint them, even after a loss or when nursing an injury. When Hull jumped to the World Hockey Association in 1972, it shook the entire sports industry. Only one player could provide the rival league instant credibility and traction: Bobby Hull. His move, rife with pressure to produce, immediately enhanced the value of players in either league.

As a Blackhawks Ambassador, Hull is as ubiquitous as he is beloved, an icon from another era. Some athletes retire and vanish from the public arena. Some say hello when it's time to say goodbye. Others, like Bobby Hull, merely show their face and merit a standing ovation. There is no expiration date on charisma. ■

**CHICAGO BLACK HAWKS 1934**

FREDERIC MCLAUGHLIN (PRES) T.P. GORMAN (MAN)
CHARLES GARDINER (CAPT) E. FROELICH (TRAIN)
TOMMY COOK   LOUIS TRUDEL   ELVIN ROMNES
JACK LESWICK   TAFFY ABEL   ROGER JENKINS
DONALD MCFADYEN   JOE STARK   WILLIAM KENDALL
HAROLD MARCH   JOHN SHEPPARD   PAUL THOMSON
ROSARIO COUTURE   LEROY GOLDSWORTHY
JOHN GOTTSELIG T CONACHER   ART COULTER

**CHICAGO BLACK HAWKS 1937-8**

FREDERIC MC LAUGHLIN (PRES) WILL TOBIN (V PRES)
THORNE DONNELLEY (SECT TREAS) WM. J. STEWART MGR
MIKE KARAKAS   EARL SEIBERT   ALEX LEVINSKY
BILL MCKENZIE   ART WIEBE   DOC ROMNES
CULLY DAHLSTROM   CARL VOSS   PAUL THOMSON
JOHNNY GOTTSELIG JACK SHILL   HAROLD MARCH
ROGER JENKINS   LOUIS TRUDELL PALAGIO
PETE PALANGIO

WHEN A TEAM WINS THE STANLEY CUP, player names are engraved on the trophy forever, and this was the first for the Blackhawks in 1934. The owner was Major Frederic McLaughlin and the coach was Tom Gorman. The star of that team was goalie Charlie Gardiner, who led the Blackhawks to playoff victories over the Montreal Canadiens and Montreal Maroons before he shut out the Detroit Red Wings 1–0 in Game 4 of a best-of-five finals. Mush March scored in the second overtime. Soon after, Gardiner died of a brain hemorrhage.

THE BLACKHAWKS WON THEIR SECOND CUP IN 1938 under coach Bill Stewart, a former referee. Despite a regular-season record of 14–25–9, they got hot in the playoffs, beating the Canadiens and New York Americans before whipping the Maple Leafs in the finals. In Game 1, goalie Mike Karakas was injured, so the Blackhawks pulled an emergency backup, Alfie Moore, out of a Toronto saloon. He won the game, and they won the series 3–1. McLaughlin stocked that team with American players, an unheard-of tactic in those days.

NAMES OF OUR 1961 CHAMPIONS ON THE STANLEY CUP, an honor that lasts forever. They just keep adding names, year after year.

AFTER WE WON THE STANLEY CUP IN 1961, I saved some mementos of that season. I can't remember keeping my shoulder pads, but here they are. I don't know exactly where they came from, but they look authentic.

THIS IS MY STANLEY CUP RING FROM 1961. One aspect of hockey that has not changed is the way players feel about earning a championship ring. Even now, when guys are making millions of dollars, players will play four seven-game series over two months without mentioning money. Playoffs are when owners pay the bills, which is fine, and when players gut it out for a Stanley Cup and a championship ring.

CHICAGO
*1929 — 1994*

DETROIT
*1927 — 1986*

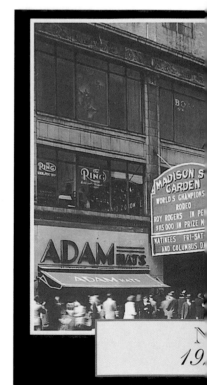

995

MONTREAL
*1924 — 1996*

RK
968

TORONTO
*1931 — 1999*

THESE ARE THE BUILDINGS WE GREW UP PLAYING IN DURING THE GREAT DAYS OF THE ORIGINAL SIX: from the left on the top row are our own Chicago Stadium, Boston Garden, and Montreal Forum; on the bottom row are the Detroit Olympia, Madison Square Garden, and Maple Leaf Gardens. Each arena was a little different. Many have been replaced by modern facilities. In the Stadium, we didn't even have an elevator or escalator.

# 15.5
## MEASUREMENT IN INCHES OF BOBBY'S BICEPS DURING HIS PLAYING CAREER.

DURING A QUIET MO-MENT AT THE STADIUM, I am putting on my sweater. I've heard a lot of stories about my strength and stamina and how experts described me as the "per-fect mesomorph," whatever that means. Players now are fanatics about conditioning, weightlifting, and nutrition, which is fine. But when I was playing, we didn't do any of that, and if I had biceps larger than Muhammad Ali's, I can assure you that had nothing to do with my spending hours pumping iron. Like my dad, I built myself up the old-fashioned way.

EARLY IN THE 1960s, I am posing in the Stadium locker room. I must have been ready for the photographer because my hair is just right.

STAN MIKITA AND I ARE ALL SCRUBBED UP HERE, grasping the Art Ross Trophy awarded to the National Hockey League scoring champion at season's end. I won three, Stan won two.

IN ACTION DURING THE 1963 NATIONAL HOCKEY LEAGUE All-Star Game at Maple Leaf Gardens. Before the current format was instituted, we started every season with an All-Star Game featuring the previous year's Stanley Cup champions against the rest of the league.

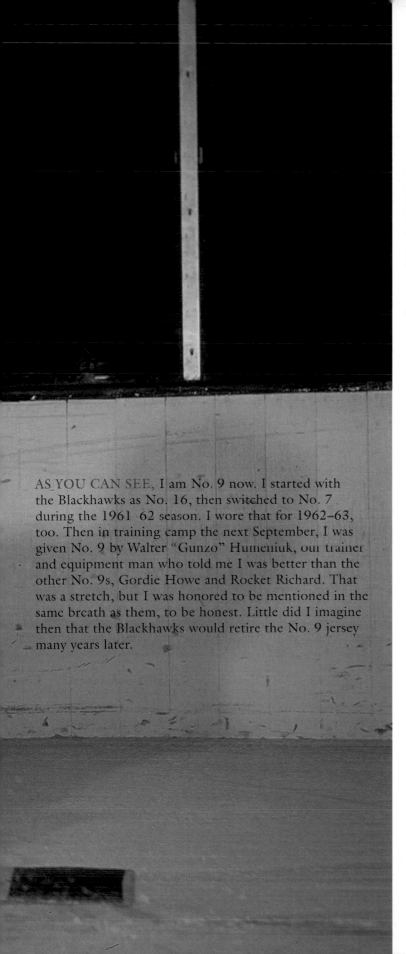

AS YOU CAN SEE, I am No. 9 now. I started with the Blackhawks as No. 16, then switched to No. 7 during the 1961–62 season. I wore that for 1962–63, too. Then in training camp the next September, I was given No. 9 by Walter "Gunzo" Humeniuk, our trainer and equipment man who told me I was better than the other No. 9s, Gordie Howe and Rocket Richard. That was a stretch, but I was honored to be mentioned in the same breath as them, to be honest. Little did I imagine then that the Blackhawks would retire the No. 9 jersey many years later.

I HAVE THE PUCK IN TOW HERE AT TORONTO'S MAPLE LEAF GARDENS during the 1963–64 season. A decent year for me, but for the Blackhawks, no Stanley Cup.

IT'S JOHNNY BOWER of the Toronto Maple Leafs against me again, at Maple Leaf Gardens, a cathedral of hockey in Canada. The fans there loved their team, but were appreciative of visiting players, too. It was always a treat to play there.

I AM AT PEACE during training camp of 1963 with the Black-hawks and my No. 9 sweater. Rocket Richard, whom I admired greatly, correctly said that "there may be 25 better stickhandlers in the NHL than Hull, but he puts the puck in the net."

THE BAY OF QUINTE was the nearest body of water to where I grew up in Point Anne, Ontario. You already know that we put it to good use in the winter when it froze over and became the neighborhood hockey rink. But in the summer, when we went back there to relax, I occasionally did some scuba diving. We weren't much for sitting around indoors, watching TV or whatever. Kids now spend hours on video games, but our young-sters need to participate in more physical activities. As a scuba diver, by the way, I made a great hockey player.

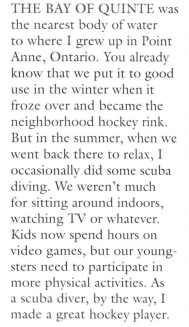

SU CASA was a popular Mexican restau-rant in Chicago during my playing days, and a lot of us went in there on a regular basis. We were always welcome. When the 2010 Blackhawks won the Cup, I thought to myself, *These guys will never have to buy another meal in this city.*

# 8

NUMBER OF GOALS BOBBY SCORED IN FIVE PLAYOFF GAMES DURING THE 1962–63 SEASON.

THIS IS ME WITH ALL OF MY HAIR—or at least most of it—which means I'm playing in the mid 1960s. By this time, our coach with the Blackhawks was Billy Reay, who was extremely supportive of me. Billy played with the Montreal Canadiens (where one of his teammates was Rocket Richard), and against Gordie Howe. But Billy was quoted as saying that "Bobby is the greatest hockey player I have ever seen. He has got size, a tremendous shot, and he loves the game." Billy was right on at least one count. I loved the game.

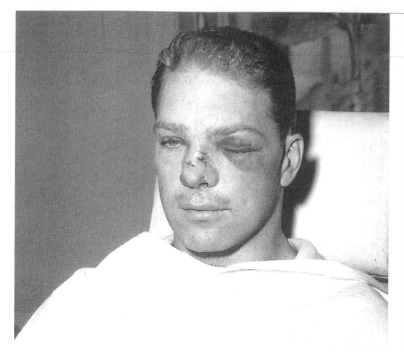

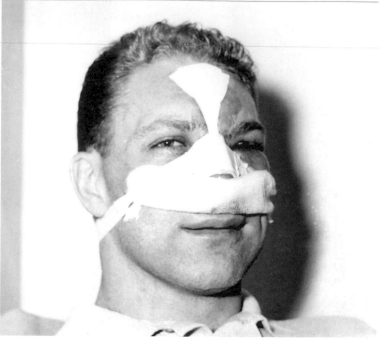

HERE'S ANOTHER LOOK AT MY PRETTY FACE after I took that stick in the face from Detroit's Bruce MacGregor during the 1963 playoffs. I scored eight goals in the series, including a hat trick in Game 6, but we were eliminated.

I LOOK LIKE SOMETHING OUT OF A HORROR MOVIE HERE. This is right after the injury I suffered when Bruce MacGregor slashed me. Playing hockey was difficult. So was breathing, eating, and sleeping.

THIS IS IN NEW YORK'S MADISON SQUARE GARDEN on December 11, 1963, after a game against the Rangers. I scored my 200th career goal against Gilles Villemure on an assist by Red Hay, and Stan Mikita tallied his 100th. We won 6–2. Stan and I prove you don't need all your teeth to celebrate.

AT THE NHL ALL-STAR GAME IN TORONTO, October 10, 1964. Gordie Howe and I were on the same team for a change, the All-Stars from the rest of the league against the Maple Leafs, who were defending Stanley Cup champions. I was No. 9 for the Blackhawks, but out of respect, I gladly took No. 7 again so Gordie could have No. 9. A bunch of Blackhawks were on the team: Glenn Hall, Moose Vasko, Pierre Pilote, and Stan Mikita.

AT PRACTICE IN THE STADIUM. I enjoyed shooting the puck, as you well know, and four nets are better than one, right?

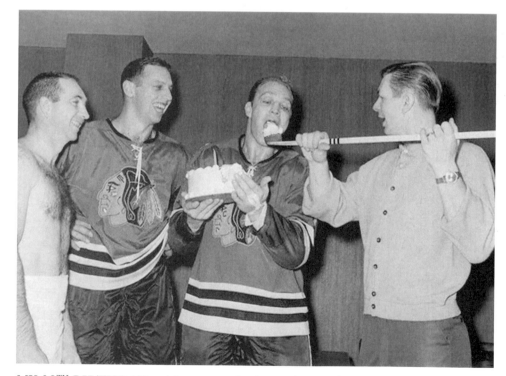

MY 28TH BIRTHDAY and I am served cake on Stan Mikita's stick, which is one way to celebrate. Kenny Wharram is at the left, brother Dennis is to my right.

I ALWAYS HAD A HIGH RESPECT FOR LAW AND ORDER. My first three friends when I moved to Chicago were police officers Bob DiPietro, "Lips" Lamonica, and Dominick Samaglia.

WE WERE ONCE FITTED FOR COWBOY HATS IN MONTREAL. The store—Chez Henri, just down the street from the Forum—took care of me, and I made sure my pals Stan Mikita, Phil Esposito, and Chico Maki also had one. Fortunately, Stan wasn't wearing his plaid pants.

I DON'T REMEMBER WHETHER THIS WAS BEFORE OR AFTER a shower with the Blackhawks. But I do know this picture was taken before women reporters started covering hockey and coming into the locker room. (*Getty Images*)

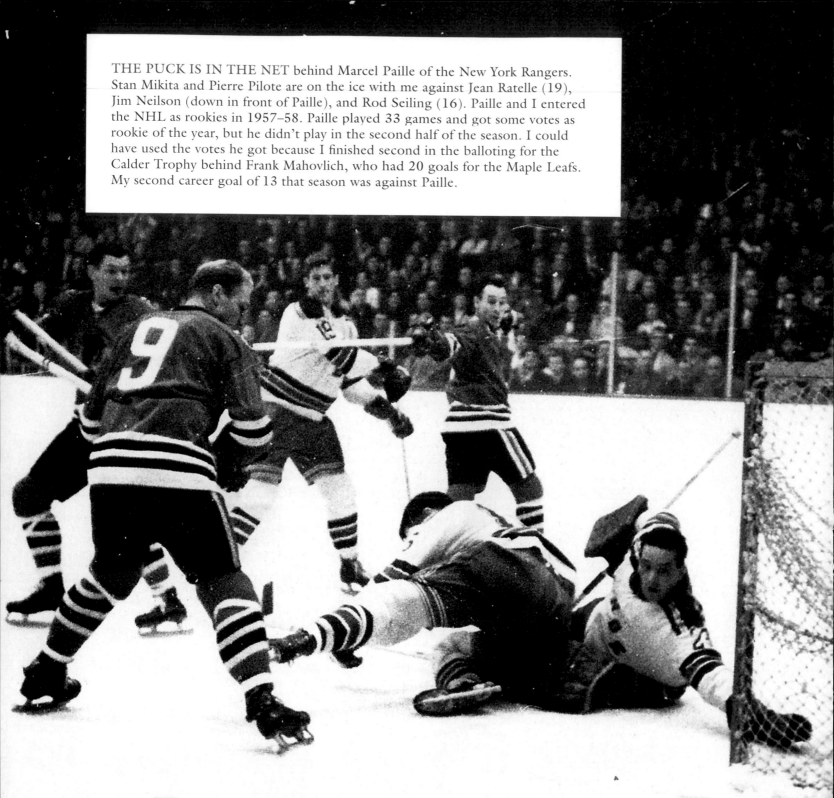

THE PUCK IS IN THE NET behind Marcel Paille of the New York Rangers. Stan Mikita and Pierre Pilote are on the ice with me against Jean Ratelle (19), Jim Neilson (down in front of Paille), and Rod Seiling (16). Paille and I entered the NHL as rookies in 1957–58. Paille played 33 games and got some votes as rookie of the year, but he didn't play in the second half of the season. I could have used the votes he got because I finished second in the balloting for the Calder Trophy behind Frank Mahovlich, who had 20 goals for the Maple Leafs. My second career goal of 13 that season was against Paille.

7 NUMBER OF TIMES BOBBY LED THE NHL IN GOALS SCORED.

I'M PITCHING during a game in Canada. It's a 16-inch softball, so I must have brought one of them back home with me from Chicago, where the sport was popular. Yes, I shot the puck left-handed, but everything else I did right-handed. That's how I signed all those autographs.

I AM PLAYING SOFTBALL at a charity game in Montreal's Jarry Park. Eat your heart out, Steve Garvey.

ON NOVEMBER 3, 1965, during a pregame presentation at the Stadium, Clarence Campbell, president of the National Hockey League, takes a business trip from his Montreal headquarters to join us. Stan Mikita won the Art Ross as leading scorer the previous season and Pierre Pilote is hoisting his third consecutive James Norris Memorial Trophy as best defenseman. I am lucky enough to have my first Hart Trophy for MVP, plus my only Lady Byng for sportsmanship combined with quality of play. I had 39 goals and 32 penalty minutes in 1964–65.

FOR THE 1965–66 SEASON, I received significant hardware. I won the Art Ross Trophy as leading scorer (54 goals, 43 assists) for the third time, just the second player in history to do so. The Hart Trophy, awarded to the most valuable player in the league, was my second in a row.

WE ARE TAKING A BREATHER BETWEEN SHIFTS on the visiting bench in Detroit's Olympia during the 1965 season. Stan Mikita is at the far left, followed to the right by Kenny Wharram, Doug Mohns, yours truly, and Chico Maki. Mohns, who could play either left wing or defense, began his career with the Boston Bruins, came to us during the summer of 1964, and turned into a pretty good scorer on a line with Stan and Kenny. Mohns had 20 goals for four straight years, including 25 in 1966–67. He had a 22-year career in the NHL.

**54**
NUMBER
OF GOALS
BOBBY
SCORED
DURING
THE 1965–66
SEASON.

POISED FOR A FACE-OFF
in the Stadium in 1965. As a
onetime center, I can tell you
that face-offs are very important, particularly in your own
zone. There's a science to
it, from studying opponents
to learning how different
officials drop the puck. Stan
Mikita was a master.

I AM HANGING OUT around one of my favorite places—the net—for this picture that was a cover for *Hockey Illustrated*, a popular magazine when I was playing. My smile is real, unlike some of my teeth, but I am a happy camper.

HERE I AM WITH PIERRE PILOTE, a great captain for the Blackhawks who would become a Hall of Fame defenseman. Pierre, like myself, was a center when he was younger, so it came naturally for him to move the puck. He was terrific at that, and he did it in an era when defensemen weren't too concerned with offense. In the mid-1950s, when the Blackhawks were really down, general manager Tommy Ivan bought the Buffalo minor league team, primarily because Pilote was there. It cost $150,000, but what a great investment that was.

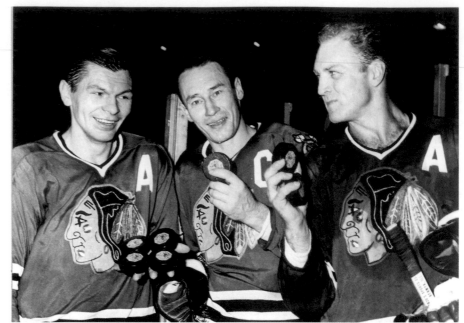

WE BEAT THE BOSTON BRUINS 7–1 ON FEBRUARY 27, 1966. Stan Mikita had four goals, Pierre Pilote one, and yours truly scored two against Bernie Parent, who wound up in the Hall of Fame after leading the Philadelphia Flyers to two Stanley Cups.

CLARENCE CAMPBELL, PRESIDENT OF THE NHL, presents the Hart Trophy to me at the start of the 1965–66 season. I scored 39 goals the previous year and was only fourth in the league in total points, but I beat out Norm Ullman of the Detroit Red Wings for the Hart. *(Getty Images)*

STAN AND I ARE DISCUSSING the curved blade in the mid-1960s. Stan cracked his stick one day in practice and noticed it had a curve in it. He took a few shots with the broken stick, and noticed that the puck acted differently, like it was moving faster. A complete accident.

PLAYERS SPENT A LOT OF TIME AROUND THE STICK RACK IN OUR DAY, checking our tools of the trade. I am looking at the curved blade here. Funny how no two sticks ever felt the same, even if they looked the same and were made by the same manufacturer.

JOHNNY BOWER, THE HALL OF FAME GOALIE for the Toronto Maple Leafs, always told me that he thought this puck was going wide. But the fact is, this puck is going to wind up in the middle of the net. The goal was my 29th of the 1964–65 season, scored in Maple Leaf Gardens on Boxing Day, which is the day after Christmas in Canada. Unfortunately, I scored only 10 more goals all season. I strained knee ligaments after a check by Bobby Baun, then took another hit from Arnie Brown of the New York Rangers.

I GOT A STANDING OVATION IN BOSTON GARDEN WHEN I SCORED MY 600TH GOAL IN 1972, but here a fan is not too happy with me during an earlier game. He's pointing and I'm chuckling. There's a glass partition between us, but I can still hear this guy loud and clear.

WHENEVER PEOPLE ASKED ME why I looked happy most of the time, especially off the ice and around our great fans, I remind them that my job was to play a game. As a kid, I always figured it was either working in a cement plant like my dad... or hockey.

WE LOST THE STANLEY CUP FINALS in seven games to the Montreal Canadiens in 1965. After the clincher in the Forum, a 4–0 victory for Montreal, I shake hands with Jean Beliveau, named the first Conn Smythe Trophy winner as most valuable player in the playoffs.

WITH MY RELIABLE TEAMMATE
CHICO MAKI nearby, I attempt to gather
in the puck. I always maintained that
skating was the most important skill in
our game, but handling the puck is a close
second. The trick is to be able to combine
both, at whatever speed, and in traffic.

ROCKY WIRTZ, SON OF BILL, was just a kid when I signed these sticks for him. I told him that one day, he would run the Blackhawks. How's that for a prediction? Rocky took over when Bill died in 2007 and has done a fabulous job of reviving the franchise.

TED WILLIAMS, arguably the greatest hitter who ever lived, and I worked for the same company, Sears, at one point. We hooked up in New York, where he and the Boston Red Sox were visiting. He was a war hero, a Hall of Famer, and a hell of a guy.

HARVEY WITTENBERG HAS BEEN A FIXTURE around the Blackhawks, as a broadcaster and public address announcer, forever. After I scored my 51st goal on March 12, 1966, Harvey interviewed me on the radio in the penalty box at the Stadium.

THIS IS ANOTHER MOMENT during the 1965 Stanley Cup Finals against the Montreal Canadiens. Jean Beliveau, their captain, is keeping tabs on me, while defenseman Ted Harris is in the background. Beliveau scored 14 seconds into Game 7, their clinching victory.

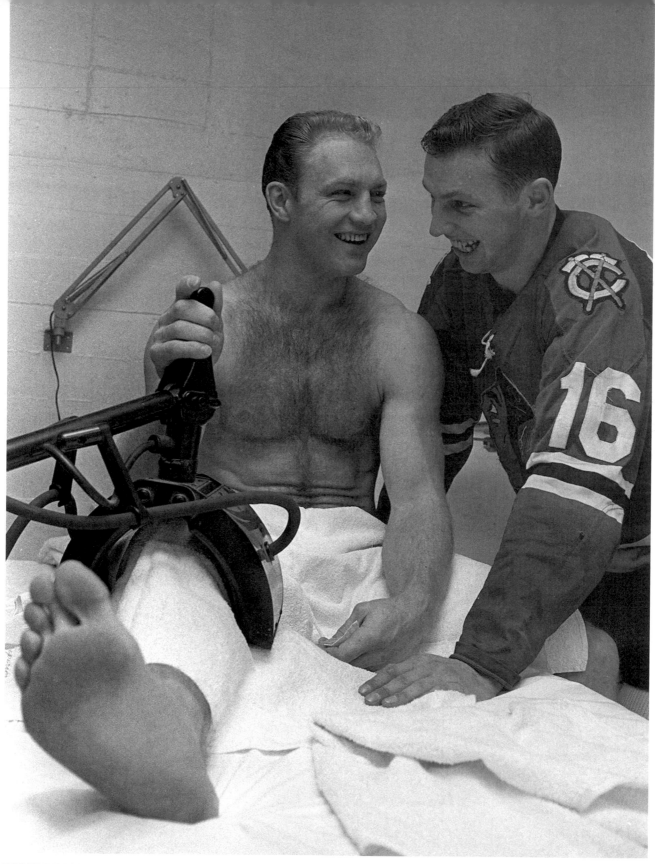

TENDING TO MY AFOREMENTIONED KNEE injury in 1965, I use really sophisticated equipment to heal while my brother Dennis observes. I missed nine games and scored only once in February and March. *(AP Images)*

GOAL NO. 337 OF MY CAREER was scored at the Detroit Olympia against Roger Crozier of the Red Wings on January 5, 1967. Ken Wharram and Stan Mikita assisted.

# ONE OF BOBBY'S SLAP SHOTS WAS ONCE MEASURED AT

# 118.3 MPH

AT THE REQUEST OF PHOTOGRAPHERS, I am hamming it up in Toronto's Maple Leaf Gardens, jumping over a stack of pucks. I believe there were 50 in the pile, and it was while I was on my way to breaking the existing record of 50 in one season shared by Maurice "Rocket" Richard and Bernie "Boom Boom" Geoffrion of the Montreal Canadiens. This bit of showmanship did not prove to be a jinx, as I scored my 51st in March of that 1965–66 season and wound up with 54. Two of those were on Christmas Night in Toronto against Terry Sawchuk, a Hall of Famer.

I DON'T KNOW FOR SURE WHERE THE PUCK IS. Maybe I've already shot it in Madison Square Garden during a game against the New York Rangers.

THIS WAS THE GOAL THAT GOT ME TO 50 in 1965–66. The puck is in the net behind Hank Bassen of the Detroit Red Wings at the Stadium. I fired a low wrist shot, just inside the right post. Kenny Wharram and Stan Mikita assisted. We won 5–4 on March 2, 1966.

AFTER THAT GAME, I was reunited with the puck in the locker room.

THIS IS IT, FOLKS! My 51st against Cesare Maniago, who happened to be in goal for Toronto when Boom Boom Geoffrion scored his 50th in 1961. On this play, Maniago said Eric Nesterenko did more than create a screen. "He lifted my stick and the shot went under it," Maniago contended.

# HULL GETS 51ST AS HAWKS END SKID, 4-2

## IT'S GOAL NO. 51 AND HULLABALOO!

### BOBBY'S 50-FOOT SLAP SHOT IN THIRD PERIOD SETS MARK

I AM SALUTING IN MY PARTY HAT after collecting my 51st goal. Two out of four pictures with my teeth in place isn't bad, right?

THIS IS ON MARCH 12, 1966, after I scored my 51st of the season against Cesare Maniago of the New York Rangers to break the single-season record. Lou Angotti and Bill Hay assisted on a power play, and we won 4–2. I had scored No. 50 10 days earlier, so I had to wait a while. When I finally got No. 51, Angotti remarked how he'd kicked the puck toward me, then gone to the bench. "I assisted on a historic goal," Angotti said, "while I was sitting down."

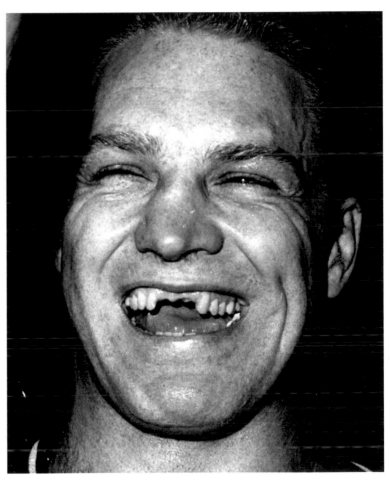

IN ADDITION TO MARKING MY 51ST GOAL with pucks, I did it with pool balls. We had a pool table beside our locker room in the Stadium, so we thought this would be a different look. I felt a lot of relief after scoring that night. After I got No. 50, we were shut out in three consecutive games—5–0 at Toronto, 1–0 against Montreal at Chicago, and then 1–0 again in New York against the Rangers. That wasn't supposed to happen. We led the NHL in goals that season. So I was probably a bit grumpy.

BUT AS YOU CAN SEE, THE MOOD PASSED. This is from the same night of No. 51, only without all my teeth. Strangely enough, before that game, I got a new batch of sticks from the manufacturer, curved blade and all. I thought they would maybe change my luck, but they just didn't feel quite right during the warm-ups, and I was thinking the same thing during much of the game. I had a few chances against Maniago, but he handled everything. In fact, the Rangers led 2–1 in the third period. Then I beat him with a slap shot while Eric Nesterenko screened.

DURING THE 1965 STANLEY CUP FINALS, we took the mighty Montreal Canadiens to the limit before losing Game 7. That made it six Stanley Cups for them in 10 years with Toe Blake as coach. As I wind up, Claude Larose is to my left and Jean Beliveau is in front. The referee is Frank Udvari, a very animated official (and a good one) who was inducted into the Hall of Fame. I had 10 goals in two seven-game play-off series that year (Detroit was the first), but only two of those goals came against the Canadiens. *(Getty Images)*

THE PUCK IS HEADING FOR THE NET behind a fallen Rozer Crozier, goalie for the Detroit Red Wings, during the 1966 playoffs. We had beaten the Red Wings the previous spring in an exciting seven-game series (before we lost the finals to Montreal, also in seven) and drew the Red Wings again in the first round the next year. My "shadow" was Bryan "Bugsy" Watson, and we lost in six games. The Red Wings lost the finals to Montreal, but Crozier was so good in defeat, he was voted the Conn Smythe Trophy winner.

# 28.3 MPH

SPEED AT WHICH BOBBY WAS ONCE MEASURED WHILE SKATING WITH THE PUCK.

IN THE MID-1960S, THE BOSTON BRUINS weren't much of a team. But that would change in a hurry because they had welcomed Bobby Orr, seen here sporting his crew cut over my right shoulder. Orr won the 1967 Calder Trophy as best rookie in the NHL, accumulating 168 of a possible 180 points, and the rest is history. He revolutionized the way defensemen played, not that anyone else could carry the puck and pass it like he did. The Bruins' best defense was him on offense. Ted Green and Tommy Williams (far right) are in the background.

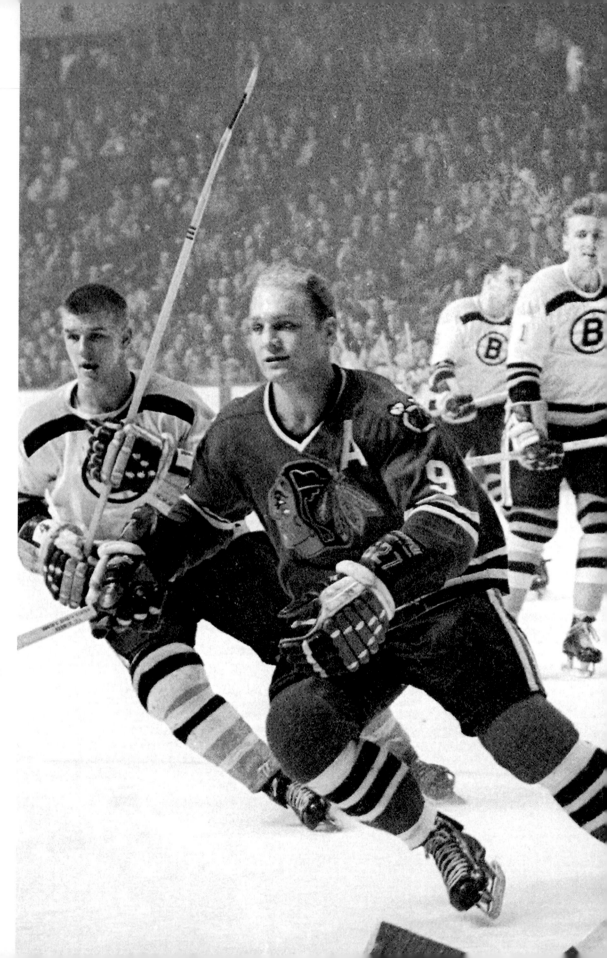

THIS PICTURE IS FROM AN ADVERTISEMENT I did to promote not smoking cigarettes. I didn't smoke then and still don't, but there were times when several of my Blackhawks teammates would light up in the locker room between periods.

I AM NOT ONLY IN CLOSE COMPANY, BUT ELITE COMPANY, as I try to deal with three members of the Toronto Maple Leafs: Allan Stanley (left), Tim Horton (7), and Red Kelly (4). All three of the men in blue are now in the Hall of Fame.

# HAWKS WIN 7-5 SHOOTOUT; 3 FOR BOBBY

ON MARCH 1, 1967, I MANAGED A HAT TRICK in the Stadium against Ed Giacomin of the New York Rangers. I had 52 goals that season, 11 of them against Giacomin. One of the guys who assisted on this night was Phil Esposito, whom the Blackhawks let get away.

## BOBBY HULL'S 28 CAREER HAT TRICKS

| NO. | DATE | GOALIE | VENUE |
|---|---|---|---|
| 1 | 12/6/1959 | Lumley | Boston Garden |
| 2 | 12/20/1959 | Chadwick | Chicago Stadium |
| 3 | 12/27/1959 | Lumley | Chicago Stadium |
| 4 | 2/21/1960 | Bower | Chicago Stadium |
| 5 | 10/9/1960 | Worsley | Chicago Stadium |
| 6 | 11/29/1961 | Head | Chicago Stadium |
| 7 | 2/1/1962 | Sawchuck | Detroit Olympia |
| 8 | 1/31/1963 | Johnston | Boston Garden |
| 9 | 2/17/1963 | Johnston | Chicago Stadium |
| 10 | 11/17/1963 | Simmons | Chicago Stadium |
| 11 | 1/11/1964 | Crozier | Chicago Stadium |
| 12 | 10/25/1964 | Paille | Madison Square Garden |
| 13 | 11/15/1964 | Bower | Chicago Stadium |
| 14 | 10/23/1965 | Bower | Maple Leaf Gardens |
| 15 | 11/7/1965 | Sawchuck | Chicago Stadium |
| 16 | 12/15/1965 | Cheevers | Chicago Stadium |
| 17 | 1/16/1966 | Maniago | Chicago Stadium |
| 18 | 1/11/1967 | Crozier | Chicago Stadium |
| 19 | 2/11/1967 | Gamble | Maple Leaf Gardens |
| 20 | 3/1/1967 | Giacomin | Chicago Stadium |
| 21 | 11/22/1967 | Giacomin | Madison Square Garden |
| 22 | 11/14/1968 | Binkley | Mellon Arena |
| 23 | 12/8/1968 | Cheevers | Chicago Stadium |
| 24 | 2/20/1969 | Caron | Great Western Forum |
| 25 | 11/22/1970 | Sneddon | Chicago Stadium |
| 26 | 2/6/1971 | Gilbert | Met Center |
| 27 | 2/21/1971 | DeJordy | Chicago Stadium |
| 28 | 12/22/1971 | Meloche | Oakland-Alameda County Coliseum Arena |

FINALLY, THE BLACK-HAWKS FINISHED FIRST IN 1967, an occasion that merited some bubbly with Lou Angotti (left) and Ken Hodge (right), whom the Blackhawks also let get away. Pierre Pilote is at far right. This ended the "Curse of Muldoon." As the story goes, after the 1926–27 season, Blackhawks owner Major Frederic McLaughlin was so upset with his team that he fired coach Pete Muldoon, who in turn was so mad that he said, "This team will never finish in first place." Well, curse or not, for four decades he was right.

AND HERE I AM with a bottle of my own, courtesy of the Wirtz family beverage business.

OWNER ARTHUR WIRTZ AND YOURS TRULY accepted the Mayor Richard J. Daley Award after we captured the Prince of Wales Trophy.

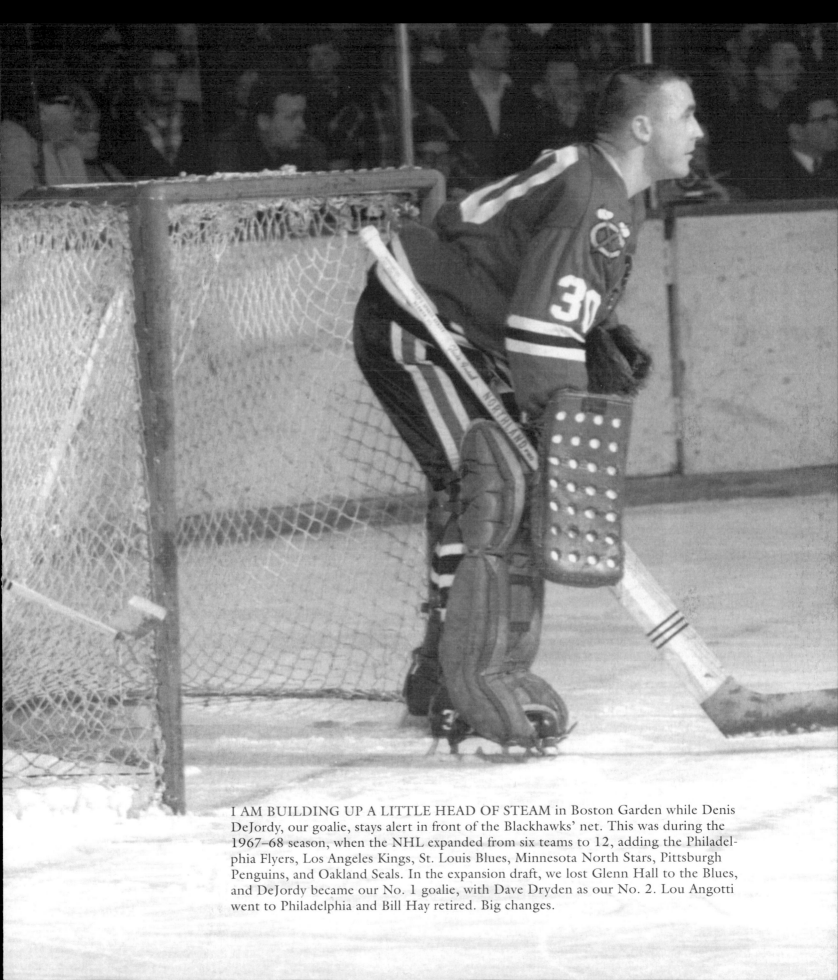

I AM BUILDING UP A LITTLE HEAD OF STEAM in Boston Garden while Denis DeJordy, our goalie, stays alert in front of the Blackhawks' net. This was during the 1967–68 season, when the NHL expanded from six teams to 12, adding the Philadelphia Flyers, Los Angeles Kings, St. Louis Blues, Minnesota North Stars, Pittsburgh Penguins, and Oakland Seals. In the expansion draft, we lost Glenn Hall to the Blues, and DeJordy became our No. 1 goalie, with Dave Dryden as our No. 2. Lou Angotti went to Philadelphia and Bill Hay retired. Big changes.

# JANUARY 7, 1968

DATE ON WHICH BOBBY SCORED HIS 400TH AND 401ST CAREER GOALS.

ALSO DURING THE 1967–68 SEASON, a year when there was a lot of movement in the NHL. I referred to the losses of Phil Esposito and Ken Hodge. The Blackhawks sent them to Boston along with Fred Stanfield in what I believe was the worst trade in hockey history. We got Gilles Marotte, Pit Martin, and goalie Jack Norris. I heard the Bruins were offering Gerry Cheevers, but the Blackhawks held out for Norris. Hard to believe.

# Hull Gets Nos. 400-1

I DID SCORE MY 400ᵀᴴ CAREER GOAL against those Bruins on January 7, 1968. Cheevers is in goal, with Dallas Smith (26) and Bobby Orr defending. With Esposito, Hodge, and Stanfield, the Bruins were building a powerhouse.

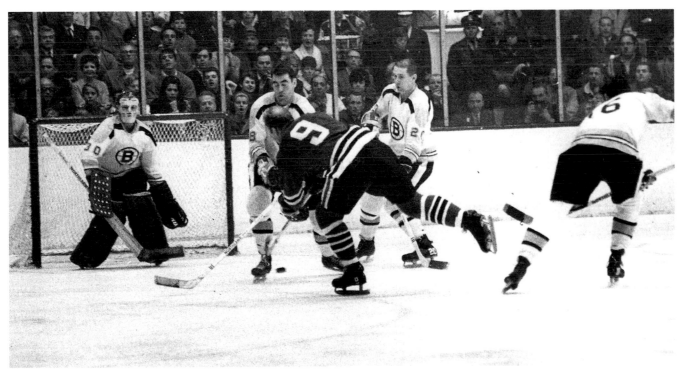

LATER IN THE SAME GAME, I notched No. 401 around Eddie Westfall and Smith. Beating Cheevers didn't change my mind; he was a good goalie, as he later proved when Boston became a winner, thanks a lot to that trade with the Blackhawks.

TOMMY IVAN, THE BLACKHAWKS' GENERAL MAN-AGER, is on the left and coach Billy Reay is on the right as we reflect on my 400th and 401st goals. To my immediate left is Michael Wirtz, brother of Bill and son of Arthur. Ivan and Reay must have had a problem with Phil Esposito, who scored 21 goals for us the previous year. So Ivan swung that trade with the Bruins, and Espo scored 35 the next year and went on to become a superstar. Hodge and Stanfield fit right in with Bobby Orr and the rest of that gang, too.

AFTER NOS. 400 AND 401, I went on to score 44 that season. That year featured a much different travel schedule as we made West Coast trips to Los Angeles and Oakland for the first time.

PITTSBURGH WAS ANOTHER NEW STOP, and in the Penguins' first year, I was wrapped up by Al MacNeil, a former Chicago teammate who joined them in the expansion draft. The goalie is Hank Bassen. Val Fonteyne, another NHL veteran, is in the background.

MY 408TH CAREER GOAL, and 38th of the 1967–68 season, was scored at the Montreal Forum on February 10 against Lorne "Gump" Worsley. A funny guy, Gump was asked when he was playing for New York which team gave him the most trouble. "The Rangers," he answered.

THIS PHOTOGRAPH WAS A *SPORTS ILLUSTRATED* COVER IN 1968. I am on the bench next to a couple of members from the "Scooter Line"—Doug Mohns to my left and Kenny Wharram to his left. As you can see, I am wearing an "A" as an alternate captain. I served in that capacity for a few years. I can't honestly remember exactly how many. It wasn't a big job. But I do know that after I sat out a few games at the start of the 1969–70 season, the "A" wasn't on my sweater when I finally settled on a contract with the Blackhawks.

THE ST. LOUIS BLUES WERE ONE OF THOSE SIX EXPANSION TEAMS that became the West Division in 1967–68, and in part because of their proximity to Chicago, the Blackhawks struck up a spirited rivalry with the Blues that still exists. You can see Scotty Bowman standing on the St. Louis bench. He began his NHL coaching career with the Blues, took them to the Stanley Cup Finals, and became a legend. When the 2010 Blackhawks won the Cup, Scotty was in their front office and his son Stan was their general manager.

IN BOSTON GARDEN ON MARCH 20, 1969. I scored two goals to reach 55 on the season, breaking my own mark of 54. Both goals were against Gerry Cheevers.

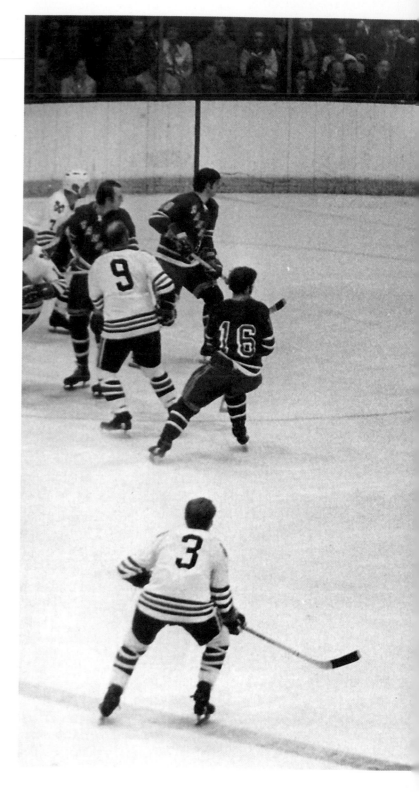

ONE OF THE GREATEST SERIES OF ALL TIME featured the Blackhawks and the New York Rangers in the 1971 Stanley Cup Semifinals. A helmeted Pit Martin won the face-off and got the puck back to me. I beat Ed Giacomin in overtime of Game 5. We won the series in seven.

# 12

NUMBER OF TIMES BOBBY WAS SELECTED FOR THE NHL ALL-STAR GAME.

ON MARCH 1, 1968, I MADE THE COVER OF *TIME* MAGAZINE, a national weekly that didn't usually devote much space to sports, let alone hockey. I was told that I was only the third hockey player to be so honored by *Time*, and the painting is the work of LeRoy Neiman, a popular contemporary artist who devoted a lot of his efforts to athletics. Neiman's theory: "For the athlete, what was fun as a kid becomes business as a pro. But still, deep down, the paying spectator never has the fun of involvement the paid athlete has."

**TIME**

**CHICAGO'S BOBBY HULL**

**Fastest Shot In the Fastest Game**

LeRoy Neiman

AT THE FORD CITY SHOPPING CENTER IN CHICAGO, I am signing Bobby Hull Hockey Games. This is a long time before the video games that kids spend time with now. No batteries required in the Bobby Hull Hockey Game.

STAN MIKITA AND I OBVIOUSLY HAVE SOME FREE TIME, so we do some arm wrestling. We took our jobs seriously, but it goes without saying that we also had a lot of laughs. Stan came to the Blackhawks a couple years after me and helped keep us loose.

GORDIE HOWE (9), JEAN BELIVEAU, AND I are on the same team for the 1968 All-Star Game in Toronto. The Maple Leafs won the Stanley Cup, so they played the rest of us. The Leafs won, but it was a treat to be on Gordie and Jean's side.

I GOT CLIPPED BY THE STICK OF MONTREAL'S JOHN FERGUSON. This looks worse than it was, but he didn't know where to draw the line. "Shadows" who were out there to throw me off my game, like Bob Nevin, Ed Westfall, and Claude Provost, I respected. Not the case with Ferguson and Bryan Watson.

I GOT STITCHED UP after getting sliced and diced in Boston Garden, but I did not miss a shift.

I HIT THE ICE FACE FIRST after being tripped by Arnie Brown, a defenseman for the New York Rangers. Shortly after I took this tumble, I scored on a power play in Madison Square Garden on February 26, 1969, against Ed Giacomin. Stan Mikita and Jim Pappin assisted, but we lost 5–3.

ALTERNATE CAPTAINS STAN MIKITA AND YOURS TRULY, with our coach, William Tulip Reay. I kid you not. He liked to be called "Billy," and that's what everybody called him. But his middle name was Tulip.

OUR ANNUAL CHRISTMAS PARTY at the Stadium in 1968. Players, families, and Santa Claus all skated, then moved downstairs. I am standing in the middle with Pierre Pilote on my left and my brother Dennis to his left.

THIS IS CAREER GOAL NO. 421 against Wayne Rutledge of the Kings in the Los Angeles Forum on October 30, 1968. The Kings were owned by Jack Kent Cooke, a Canadian. Rumor has it he tried to trade for me before I jumped to the World Hockey Association in 1972.

OUR EQUIPMENT MAN-AGER, Don "Socko" Uren, is handling the honors of fitting me with a protective helmet after I broke my jaw on Christmas Night in 1968. I missed one game while playing six weeks with a wired jaw.

MY NOURISHMENT during that time was described by one writer as "brownish ugh," which is pretty much how it tasted, too. My meals went into a blender before I "ate" and they were no substitute for a steak, that's for sure.

JUST TO PROVE I COULD STILL CONTRIBUTE with a helmet on, I scored on January 8, 1969, against goalie Jacques Plante, the former Montreal Canadiens great who had moved on to the St. Louis Blues. Wearing my headgear and sipping my brownish ugh through a straw, I managed to score 10 goals. "Watch out when he gets rid of that thing," suggested my brother Dennis. "Bobby will be like a bird just freed from a cage." With solid food and my vision no longer obscured, I was able to collect 19 goals in my first 14 games minus the helmet.

IT ISN'T EVERY DAY THAT YOU SMILE when you have an appointment with the doctor, but on this red-letter day in 1969 the wires were removed from my jaw, now healed. I could eat real food again! My son Brett doesn't seem too excited, but let me assure you, I was.

MY HELMET AND I SCORE against Gerry Desjardins of the Los Angeles Kings at the Stadium on January 12, 1969, while defenseman Dale Rolfe trails the play. I wound up scoring twice that night in a 4–2 victory to reach the 30-goal mark for the season. As brother Dennis predicted, I went on a bit of a binge when I got healthy and finished with 58 goals. But, as I said, we wound up in last place, and the next season, we underwent some big changes. One of them was the acquisition of Desjardins to beef up our goalkeeping.

THIS WAS MY 49TH OF THE 1968–69 SEASON, with Ed Giacomin in goal for the visiting New York Rangers. It was a strange year. I mentioned that we finished in sixth and last place in the East despite having a winning record. What's worse, my former linemate, Phil Esposito, went crazy in Boston with 49 goals and 77 assists for 126 points, easily the most in the NHL. When I said letting him go to the Bruins was the worst trade in hockey history, I wasn't kidding.

ON MARCH 5, 1969, I REGISTERED MY 50TH GOAL at the Stadium against Ed Giacomin of the New York Rangers. Earlier in the same game, a 4–4 tie, I got my 49th. Both goals were assisted by Chico Maki and Andre Boudrias. I went over to shake hands with Bill Wirtz, son of our owner, Arthur. It was the fourth time I had scored 50 in one season, a record that I would stretch to five in 1971–72.

AFTER I SCORED 50 GOALS for the fourth time in March of 1969, I marked the occasion with sticks and pucks.

MY 58TH AND LAST GOAL OF THE SAME SEASON, on March 30, 1969, against Roger Crozier and the Detroit Red Wings at the Stadium. Gilles Marotte and Pat Stapleton assisted as we romped 9–5.

I WIND UP WITH THE PUCK at Boston Garden, a rink that was slightly smaller than ours at the Stadium. Not all arenas had equal dimensions then, although the differences might not have been noticeable to the naked eye. I can tell you that those Bruins fans could usually be heard. They were right on top of you in that building, and they often had some pithy remarks. I can't complain about how they treated me. They were great. With Bobby Orr and Phil Esposito to watch, those people started packing the place again. The Bruins won the Stanley Cup in 1970 and 1972.

GORDIE HOWE AND I are mucking it up along the boards, something we did often. After I jumped to the World Hockey Association, Gordie showed up there, too. He played forever.

STAN MIKITA IS POINTING AT MY LEFT KNEE in practice. I might have injured it somehow, but I don't appear to be hurting. Maybe Stan was just looking for a laugh.

ONE REASON WE WENT FROM LAST TO FIRST in 1969–70 was our rookie goalie, Tony Esposito, stolen from the Montreal Canadiens for $25,000. I celebrated his 15th shutout with Gerry Pinder. Tony O's mark still stands as a modern record. He was on his way to the Hall of Fame.

# HULL NETS 500TH AS HAWKS WIN, 4 TO 2

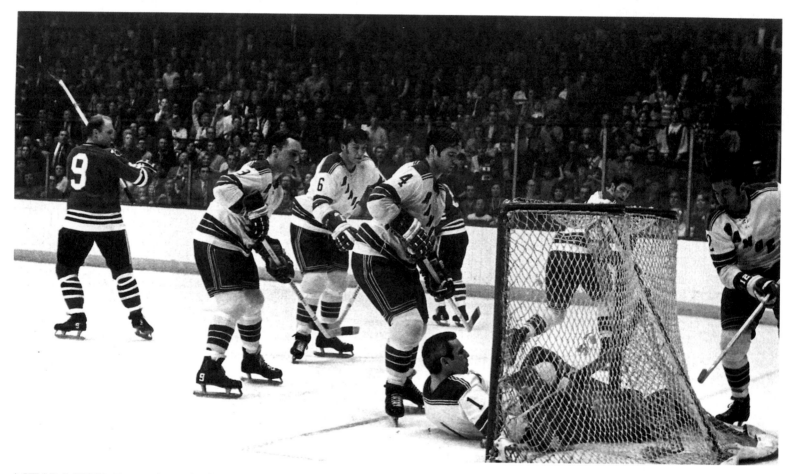

A YEAR LATER, I scored my 500th career goal in the Stadium, my second of the night against Ed Giacomin on February 21, 1970. Bill White assisted on my 500th in his first game with the Blackhawks, who acquired him from Los Angeles in a very good trade.

LOU ANGOTTI (LEFT) AND BILL WHITE (SEATED) help celebrate their assists on my 500th career goal. White had just arrived from the Kings and instantly fit in as a stay-at-home defensive partner with Pat Stapleton to form one of the best blue-line tandems in the league.

AT THE TIME, only two other men had scored 500 goals: Maurice Richard and Gordie Howe.

GORDIE HOWE AND ME at the 1970 NHL All-Star Game in St. Louis, where I assisted on his goal and got one myself as the East defeated the West 4–3. It was nice having Gordie on my side for a change. He was no fun to play against.

AT THE 1971 ALL-STAR GAME in Boston, after the Bruins had won the Stanley Cup the previous year, I am joined by my brother Dennis (10) and goalie Tony Esposito (35), as well as Phil Esposito, my former teammate and then a Bruins superstar.

THIS IS THE 1970 ALL-STAR GAME IN ST. LOUIS. The Brothers Esposito, Tony and Phil, one a goalie and one a forward, had two different personalities. A couple of beauties, believe me. Hall of Famers both, and lots of fun.

THERE'S NOT MUCH MORE I CAN SAY ABOUT NO. 4, BOBBY ORR, other than he was the greatest player I ever played against, without question, and by quite a margin. With all due respect to others, Bobby did it all. He won scoring titles as an offensive defenseman, he won Hart Trophies as most valuable player in the league, and he won eight straight Norris Trophies as the best at his position. He left the Bruins in 1976 for the Blackhawks, but his knee was shot and he retired at 30. What a shame. He might still be playing otherwise, and he's over 60.

# Bobby Blasts 544th to

# Beat Penguins

ON FEBRUARY 7, 1971, I SCORED MY 544TH CAREER GOAL at the Stadium to tie Maurice "Rocket" Richard's mark with the Montreal Canadiens. Les Binkley was the goalie, and Syl Apps is checking me. We won 1–0. Richard became the NHL's all-time leading goal scorer when he scored his 325th in 1952 to pass Nels Stewart. Gordie Howe, who retired from the Detroit Red Wings in 1971 but eventually played in the WHA, passed Richard. Being mentioned in the same breath as both of them was an honor. Don't forget, when he retired in 1960, Richard had another 82 playoff goals.

THIS IS THE GOAL that put me past the Rocket. Charlie Hodge of the Vancouver Canucks tried to stop it with his glove. Gerry Pinder (18) and Bryan Campbell (14), each of whom assisted on the goal, are to the left. The Blackhawks were on a power play.

# BEAT CANUCKS

ON FEBRUARY 14, 1971, in a game against the Vancouver Canucks, I passed Maurice "Rocket" Richard with my 545th and 546th goals to become the second-all-time leading goal scorer in NHL history. Charlie Hodge was the goalie in a 3–1 victory for us at the Stadium.

I HAD AN EXCELLENT RELATIONSHIP WITH THE PRESS as a player, particularly these three old pros in Chicago: Ed Sainsbury (left), Red Mottlow (with microphone), and Joe Mooshil. Cooperating with reporters was part of our responsibility as players. Remember, we're entertainers.

STAN MIKITA AND I ARE CLOWNING it up while signing autographs at a furniture store in Chicago. We didn't wear our teeth during this appearance, but Stan did wear one of his typically loud shirts. He probably had pants to match. That is some shirt, isn't it?

I AM ATTEMPTING TO SHAKE JEAN BELIVEAU of the Montreal Canadiens, against whom we had so many pitched battles when I was with the Blackhawks. If you don't think NHL hockey was a tough business, check out my sweater. It looks like it hasn't been to the laundry in a couple weeks, but don't blame our equipment guys. I've contributed some blood to that garment, and the rest of those marks probably came from opposing sticks. You could do things then to slow players down that aren't allowed anymore by the modern NHL rules. *(Getty Images)*

I SHED THIS BLOOD courtesy of Bryan "Bugsy" Watson, who played his version of hockey with the Detroit Red Wings—which meant doing whatever it took to "shadow" me.

I BEAT REGGIE JACKSON TO THE CANDY BAR. Here I am chowing down on the Golden Jet Candy Bar. You won't find them in your stores today.

BOBBY ORR CAME INTO THE NHL with a crew cut, but he grew a full head of hair before long. That makes one of us. As I've said, I was relatively fortunate as far as my health was concerned. In 15 years with the Blackhawks, I never played fewer than 61 games in a season, and I went that low only twice. Orr wasn't so lucky. He played only nine full seasons with the Bruins and played when he was hurt. But in his 10th season, he was able to play only 10 games. In 1976, he went to the Blackhawks, but played only 26 games for them before he had to quit.

ONE OF MY LAST GREAT MEMORIES of 15 years with the Blackhawks occurred in the Boston Garden on March 25, 1972, when I scored my 600th career goal. Gerry Cheevers tried to make a glove save, but the puck is in the net. And I shot it past royalty, because that's Bobby Orr on his knees in front of me. Brother Dennis and Pit Martin assisted on the power play, and we tied the Bruins 5–5.

IN BOSTON, AFTER NO. 600 on March 25, 1972. At this point in what was to be my last season with the Blackhawks, I had been talking to management about another contract. But I didn't get an offer until it was too late. Meanwhile, the owners of the WHA teams had agreed to pool their money and give me a $1 million signing bonus, in addition to my deal with the Winnipeg Jets. The Blackhawks contended that they couldn't pool resources because such a tactic wasn't legal. When the Blackhawks finally offered me a contract after the season, I had already given Winnipeg my word. I was gone.

MY LAST GOAL with the Blackhawks on April 2, 1972, against Andy Brown of the Detroit Red Wings. I got two that day. Coach Billy Reay is with me in the locker room. Here's some trivia, though. I actually wound up with 610 NHL goals because I scored six with the Jets and Hartford Whalers after they became part of the league in 1979–80. My 604 goals ranked second only to Gordie Howe in NHL history at the time, but since then, I've been passed by a lot of guys, including Wayne Gretzky and my son Brett.

I AM DRIVING THE NO. 9 HORSE, G.T. WINTER, at Balmoral Park in Chicago during the summer I left the Blackhawks for Winnipeg. I look like I know what I'm doing, don't I? I won, probably because I didn't have Bugsy Watson hanging on me.

THE 1957–58 BLACKHAWKS, my rookie year. I am in the top row, second from the right, looking very happy to be in the NHL, which I was. Tommy Ivan, seated in the jacket, was our general manager and coach.

THE 1958–59 BLACKHAWKS. I am the third player from the left in the top row, next to Ted Lindsay on my right and Ron Murphy on my left.

WE MADE THE PLAYOFFS FOR A SECOND STRAIGHT YEAR IN 1960 and got swept in the first round by the Montreal Canadiens, but there was a feeling within the organization that we were building toward something special.

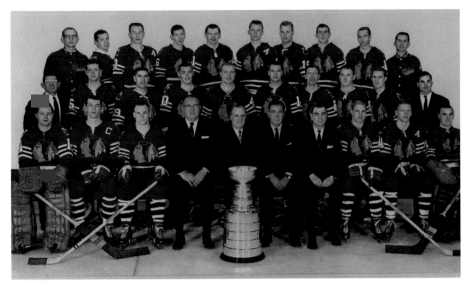

OUR 1961 STANLEY CUP CHAMPIONS. I am third from the right, next to coach Rudy Pilous. To his right are co-owner James Norris, general manager Tommy Ivan, and co-owner Arthur Wirtz. We won the Cup in Detroit and got held over because of a snowstorm. When we reached Chicago, there was an escort of fire trucks and a lot of people. Then we went to Mayor Daley's office, where Bill Hay said, "Hi, Dick. How the hell are you?" Our next stop was the Bismarck Hotel, owned by the Wirtz family. Then we went for pizza at whatever hour. I never did drink from the Cup in 1961 like they do now, nor did we get to have it for one day each.

SOME CHANGES WERE MADE AFTER OUR CUP SEASON. Ed Litzenberger was gone, for one. We finished third, won in the first round of the playoffs against Montreal, but lost the finals to Toronto.

ANOTHER SEASON WHEN I THOUGHT WE HAD ENOUGH TO WIN A STANLEY CUP, but we didn't. We finished second, then didn't get past Detroit in the semifinals.

FOR THE 1963–64 SEASON, we had a new coach, Billy Reay, standing at the far right of the middle row. I am second from the left, seated, with goalie Denis DeJordy to my right and the brass to my left. Glenn Hall is at the far right of that row, beside our captain, Pierre Pilote. Stan Mikita is fourth from the right on the top row. Second in is John McKenzie, another guy we let escape to Boston. We finished in second place that season and were eliminated in the first round of the playoffs by Detroit in seven games.

IN 1964–65 we had some new faces, including Dennis Hull, fifth from the left in the top row. He joined his brother, yours truly, who is second from the left at the bottom. Doug Mohns, second from the left in the middle row, also came aboard. During the season, we also acquired Camille Henry from the New York Rangers, where he was their captain. Stan Mikita, on Dennis' right, won the scoring title. We took third place, beat Detroit in the opening round of the playoffs, then lost the finals to Montreal. Both series went the limit.

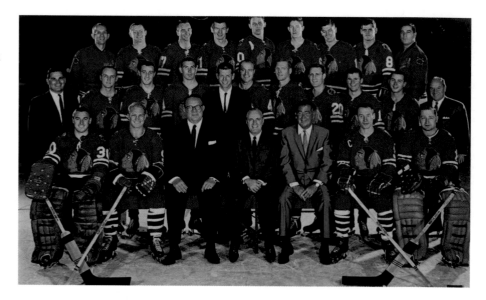

THE 1965–66 SQUAD again finished in second place, again played the Red Wings in the playoffs, and we were defeated in six games. Ken Hodge, third from the right in the middle row, joined our lineup, as did Pat Stapleton, who would become an outstanding defenseman. Stan Mikita (second from right, bottom row) and I used our curved stick blades, or "banana" blades, to enjoy a productive season. I guess we were credited with inventing the curved stick, which helped you shoot the puck and could fool goalies. But it didn't do much for the backhand.

FINALLY, we finished first during the regular season in 1966–67, refuting the so-called "Curse of Muldoon." This was the last year of the Original Six before the NHL expanded to a dozen franchises, and we celebrated it the right way. We not only captured the Prince of Wales Trophy for winding up on top, but we potted 264 goals in 70 games, a league record. I had 52 of them, Stan Mikita won the scoring race, and my brother Dennis came into his own, scoring 25. We ended on a sour note, however, being upset in the playoffs by the Maple Leafs.

IN 1967–68, the six original franchises were put in one division and the six expansion teams in another with the guarantee that the survivor of the latter, the West, would be in the Stanley Cup Finals. If you're looking for Phil Esposito, Fred Stanfield, and Ken Hodge, they aren't there. They were traded to Boston. Also, we lost Glenn Hall to the St. Louis Blues in the expansion draft. Our goalies were Denis DeJordy, to my left in the bottom row, and Dave Dryden, on the right of Stan Mikita, same row. Stan won the Ross, Hart, and Lady Byng trophies.

NOW IT'S THE 1968–69, a season during which I scored 58 goals and we had a winning record, but still finished last in the East. Bill Wirtz is on my right in the front row, and goalie Denis DeJordy is on my left.

A LOT OF NEW BLOOD ON THIS TEAM, including rookies Keith Magnuson and Tony Esposito. We had ended up in dead last the previous season, but took first this year on the final night of the regular season.

QUITE A COLLECTION OF TALENT ON THIS TEAM that finished first in the West Division with 107 points, then knocked off the Rangers in a classic series before we had our hearts broken in Game 7 of the finals at the Stadium against Montreal.

MY SWAN SONG WITH THE BLACKHAWKS. We scored a bunch of goals, we had Tony O in the nets, but we got skunked in the second round by the Rangers after sweeping Pittsburgh.

IN 1972, I AM PLAYING ONE OF MY FINAL GAMES for the Blackhawks. I left Chicago with a lot of cherished memories and friendships. In the beginning, hockey didn't feel like a business. As kids, before Stan Mikita and I married our wives, we lived together in Berwyn, a suburb of Chicago. With Tod Sloan and Ron Murphy, we each chipped in $50 to buy a 1949 Pontiac that had holes in the floorboard. We patched them up with cardboard and drove that thing until it wouldn't go anymore. Then we just left it on a street corner somewhere.

## "MR. CHARISMA: THE MAN WHO IS LOVED BY THE CROWD"

Most hockey players seem as alike
As leave on the trees,
As alike as the bees in the swarming of bees;
And we look at the thousands who have put on their skates,
All equally small and equally great;
Then fate called for a man who was larger than men,
There were many pretenders,
A scuffle and then,
There arises a man that is larger than men,
The man who is loved by the crowd.
Then the great game called out for the great man to come,
And the crowds no longer sat sullen and dumb,
And the great deeds were done for the great man did come,
The man who was loved by the crowd.

—*A poem written by my brother Dennis for yours truly*

MY 1,000TH POINT WAS AN ASSIST on a goal by brother Dennis, who was a pretty fair hockey player himself, even though he loves to make fun of himself. This happened on December 13, 1969, against an old rival, Gump Worsley, who was then playing goal for the Minnesota North Stars.

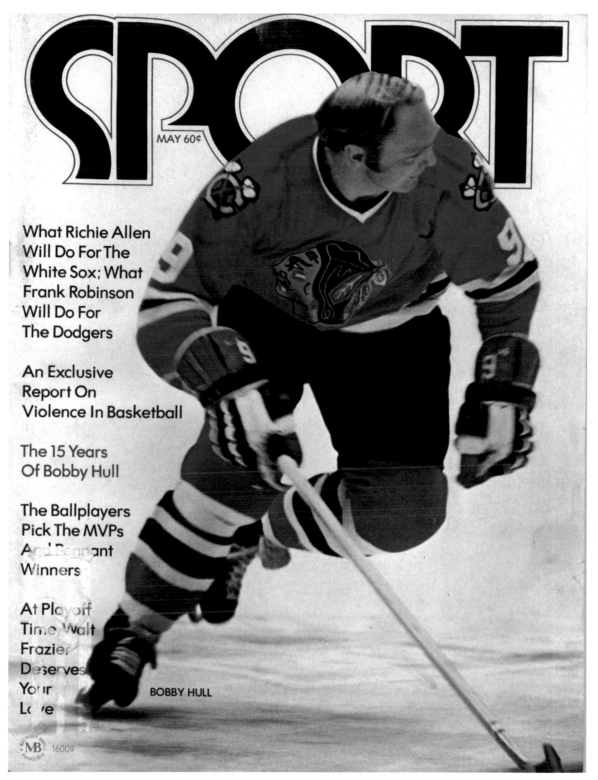

# SPORT

MAY 60¢

What Richie Allen
Will Do For The
White Sox; What
Frank Robinson
Will Do For
The Dodgers

An Exclusive
Report On
Violence In Basketball

The 15 Years
Of Bobby Hull

The Ballplayers
Pick The MVPs
And Pennant
Winners

At Playoff
Time, Walt
Frazier
Deserves
Your
Love

BOBBY HULL

MB 16009

*SPORT* MAGAZINE ISN'T AROUND ANYMORE, and shortly after this issue appeared, I wasn't around Chicago anymore, either. May of 1972 is when I jumped to the Winnipeg Jets of the World Hockey Association. "The 15 Years of Bobby Hull" on the cover referred to my 15 years with the Blackhawks.

# Bobby Hull's 604 Career Blackhawks Goals

### 1957–58
1 Oct. 22 Bos. Simmons
2 Nov. 9 N.Y. Paille
3 Nov. 10 Tor. Chadwick
4 Dec. 7 Bos. Simmons
5 Dec. 14 Tor. Chadwick
6 Jan. 12 Mon. Plante
7 Jan. 26 N.Y. Worsley
8 Feb. 6 Bos. Lumley
9 Feb. 6 Bos. Lumley
10 Mar. 12 N.Y. Worsley
11 Mar. 12 N.Y. Worsley
12 Mar. 22 Det. Sawchuk
13 Mar. 22 Det. Sawchuk

### 1958–59
14 Oct. 11 Tor. Bower
15 Oct. 12 Tor. Bower
16 Oct. 19 Bos. Simmons
17 Oct. 28 Mon. Plante
18 Oct. 28 Mon. Plante
19 Nov. 8 Det. Sawchuk
20 Nov. 16 Det. Sawchuk
21 Nov. 19 Bos. Simmons
22 Nov. 23 Tor. Bower
23 Dec. 27 Tor. Chadwick
24 Dec. 31 Det. Sawchuk
25 Jan. 4 Bos. Simmons
26 Feb. 7 N.Y. Worsley
27 Feb. 8 Tor. Chadwick
28 Feb. 15 Bos. Simmons
29 Feb. 28 Bos. Simmons
30 Feb. 28 Bos. Simmons
31 Mar. 11 N.Y. Worsley

### 1959–60
32 Oct. 7 N.Y. Worsley
33 Oct. 10 Tor. Bower
34 Oct. 15 Det. Sawchuk
35 Oct. 25 N.Y. Worsley
36 Nov. 8 Bos. Lumley
37 Nov. 10 Tor. Bower
38 Nov. 14 Tor. Bower
39 Nov. 18 N.Y. Worsley
40 Nov. 18 N.Y. Worsley
41 Nov. 28 N.Y. Paille
42 Dec. 2 Bos. Lumley
43 Dec. 6 Bos. Lumley
44 Dec. 6 Bos. Lumley
45 Dec. 6 Bos. Lumley
46 Dec. 13 Mon. Plante
47 Dec. 17 Det. Sawchuk
48 Dec. 20 Tor. Chadwick
49 Dec. 20 Tor. Chadwick
50 Dec. 20 Tor. Chadwick
51 Dec. 27 Bos. Lumley
52 Dec. 27 Bos. Lumley
53 Dec. 27 Bos. Lumley
54 Jan. 1 Det. Sawchuk
55 Jan. 2 Tor. Bower
56 Jan. 13 Det. Sawchuk
57 Jan. 17 N.Y. Worsley
58 Jan. 20 Bos. Lumley
59 Jan. 23 N.Y. Worsley
60 Feb. 14 Mon. Plante
61 Feb. 21 Tor. Bower
62 Feb. 21 Tor. Bower
63 Feb. 21 Tor. Bower
64 Feb. 21 Tor. Bower
65 Feb. 28 Det. Sawchuk
66 Feb. 28 Det. Sawchuk
67 Mar. 3 Bos. Simmons
68 Mar. 5 N.Y. Rollins
69 Mar. 13 Det. Sawchuk
70 Mar. 20 Bos. Simmons

### 1960–61
71 Oct. 6 Det. Sawchuk
72 Oct. 9 N.Y. Worsley
73 Oct. 9 N.Y. Worsley
74 Oct. 9 N.Y. Worsley
75 Oct. 12 Tor. Bower
76 Oct. 16 Bos. Simmons
77 Oct. 30 Det. Sawchuk
78 Nov. 9 Tor. Bower
79 Nov. 13 Det. Sawchuk
80 Nov. 17 Bos. Simmons
81 Nov. 27 N.Y. Worsley
82 Dec. 4 Mon. Hodge
83 Dec. 4 Mon. Hodge
84 Dec. 10 Tor. Bower
85 Dec. 10 Tor. Bower
86 Dec. 11 Tor. Bower
87 Jan. 4 N.Y. Worsley
88 Jan. 5 Bos. Gamble
89 Jan. 8 Tor. Bower
90 Jan. 11 Det. Bassen
91 Jan. 15 N.Y. Worsley
92 Jan. 22 Bos. Gamble
93 Jan. 22 Bos. Gamble
94 Feb. 8 Det. Sawchuk
95 Feb. 15 N.Y. Worsley
96 Feb. 22 N.Y. Worsley
97 Feb. 26 Bos. Gamble
98 Feb. 26 Bos. Gamble
99 Mar. 5 Tor. Maniago
100 Mar. 12 Mon. Plante
101 Mar. 15 Det. Sawchuk

### 1961–62
102 Oct. 17 Bos. Head
103 Oct. 19 N.Y. Worsley
104 Oct. 29 Bos. Head
105 Nov. 7 Tor. Bower
106 Nov. 19 Mon. Plante
107 Nov. 26 Det. Sawchuk
108 Nov. 29 Bos. Head
109 Nov. 29 Bos. Head
110 Nov. 29 Bos. Head
111 Dec. 6 N.Y. Worsley
112 Dec. 13 Bos. Chadwick
113 Dec. 17 N.Y. Worsley
114 Dec. 25 Tor. Bower
115 Dec. 30 Mon. Plante
116 Jan. 3 N.Y. Worsley
117 Jan. 11 Bos. Head
118 Jan. 13 N.Y. Worsley
119 Jan. 13 N.Y. Worsley
120 Jan. 17 Mon. Plante
121 Jan. 17 Mon. Plante
122 Jan. 24 Tor. Bower
123 Jan. 27 Bos. Gamble
124 Jan. 27 Bos. Gamble
125 Jan. 28 N.Y. Worsley
126 Jan. 28 N.Y. Worsley
127 Jan. 31 Det. Sawchuk
128 Feb. 1 Det. Sawchuk
129 Feb. 1 Det. Sawchuk
130 Feb. 1 Det. Sawchuk
131 Feb. 1 Det. Sawchuk
132 Feb. 8 Bos. Gamble
133 Feb. 8 Bos. Gamble
134 Feb. 11 Mon. Plante
135 Feb. 14 N.Y. Paille
136 Feb. 17 Mon. Plante
137 Feb. 21 Det. Bassen
138 Feb. 21 Det. Bassen
139 Feb. 24 Det. Sawchuk
140 Feb. 25 Bos. Gamble
141 Feb. 28 Tor. Bower
142 Mar. 1 Bos. Gamble
143 Mar. 1 Bos. Gamble
144 Mar. 4 Mon. Plante
145 Mar. 11 Tor. Simmons

146 Mar. 15 Mon. Plante
147 Mar. 15 Mon. Plante
148 Mar. 17 Mon. Simmons
149 Mar. 20 Det. Bassen
150 Mar. 24 Mon. Plante
151 Mar. 25 N.Y. Worsley

### 1962–63
152 Oct. 20 Tor. Bower
153 Nov. 4 Det. Sawchuk
154 Nov. 14 Det. Sawchuk
155 Nov. 14 Det. Sawchuk
156 Nov. 17 N.Y. Worsley
157 Nov. 17 N.Y. Worsley
158 Nov. 29 Bos. Perreault
159 Dec. 1 Mon. Plante
160 Dec. 22 Mon. Plante
161 Dec. 29 Tor. Bower
162 Jan. 1 Det. Sawchuk
163 Jan. 12 N.Y. Worsley
164 Jan. 19 Tor. Simmons
165 Jan. 19 Tor. Simmons
166 Jan. 20 N.Y. Worsley
167 Jan. 26 Det. Bassen
168 Jan. 31 Bos. Johnston
169 Jan. 31 Bos. Johnston
170 Jan. 31 Bos. Johnston
171 Feb. 2 Mon. Maniago
172 Feb. 3 Tor. Simmons
173 Feb. 3 Tor. Simmons
174 Feb. 9 N.Y. Worsley
175 Feb. 10 N.Y. Worsley
176 Feb. 16 Mon. Plante
177 Feb. 17 Bos. Johnston
178 Feb. 17 Bos. Johnston
179 Feb. 17 Bos. Johnston
180 Feb. 21 Det. Bassen
181 Feb. 21 Det. Bassen
182 Mar. 6 N.Y. Worsley

### 1963–64
183 Oct. 10 Det. Sawchuk
184 Oct. 13 Tor. Simmons
185 Oct. 16 Bos. Johnston
186 Oct. 26 Mon. Worsley
187 Oct. 27 N.Y. Plante
188 Nov. 2 Tor. Bower
189 Nov. 5 N.Y. Plante
190 Nov. 13 Bos. Johnston
191 Nov. 13 Bos. Johnston
192 Nov. 17 Tor. Simmons
193 Nov. 17 Tor. Simmons
194 Nov. 17 Tor. Simmons
195 Nov. 20 Det. Sawchuk
196 Nov. 20 Det. Sawchuk
197 Dec. 1 N.Y. Plante
198 Dec. 4 Bos. Johnston
199 Dec. 8 Mon. Hodge
200 Dec. 11 N.Y. Villemure
201 Dec. 21 Mon. Hodge
202 Dec. 22 Bos. Johnston
203 Dec. 25 Mon. Hodge
204 Jan. 1 N.Y. Plante
205 Jan. 5 Bos. Johnston
206 Jan. 9 Det. Crozier
207 Jan. 11 Det. Crozier
208 Jan. 11 Det. Crozier
209 Jan. 11 Det. Crozier
210 Jan. 12 Mon. Hodge
211 Jan. 18 N.Y. Plante
212 Jan. 18 N.Y. Plante
213 Jan. 25 Det. Sawchuk
214 Jan. 26 Mon. Hodge
215 Jan. 29 Det. Crozier
216 Feb. 12 N.Y. Plante
217 Feb. 16 Bos. Johnston
218 Feb. 23 Bos. Johnston
219 Feb. 27 Det. Sawchuk

220 Mar. 4 N.Y. Plante
221 Mar. 5 Bos. Johnston
222 Mar. 8 Tor. Simmons
223 Mar. 15 Det. Sawchuk
224 Mar. 17 N.Y. Plante
225 Mar. 17 N.Y. Plante

### 1964–65
226 Oct. 17 Det. Crozier
227 Oct. 21 Mon. Hodge
228 Oct. 25 N.Y. Paille
229 Oct. 25 N.Y. Paille
230 Oct. 25 N.Y. Paille
231 Oct. 31 Tor. Sawchuk
232 Nov. 1 Bos. Johnston
233 Nov. 3 N.Y. Paille
234 Nov. 15 Tor. Bower
235 Nov. 15 Tor. Bower
236 Nov. 15 Tor. Bower
237 Nov. 18 Det. Crozier
238 Nov. 18 Det. Crozier
239 Nov. 22 Mon. Hodge
240 Nov. 26 Tor. Sawchuk
241 Nov. 29 Bos. Johnston
242 Nov. 29 Bos. Johnston
243 Dec. 5 Mon. Hodge
244 Dec. 5 Mon. Hodge
245 Dec. 6 N.Y. Paille
246 Dec. 10 Bos. Johnston
247 Dec. 12 Det. Crozier
248 Dec. 13 Det. Crozier
249 Dec. 16 Bos. Johnston
250 Dec. 16 Bos. Johnston
251 Dec. 19 Mon. Hodge
252 Dec. 19 Mon. Hodge
253 Dec. 20 Bos. Johnston
254 Dec. 26 Tor. Bower
255 Dec. 29 N.Y. Plante
256 Dec. 29 N.Y. Plante
257 Jan. 3 Mon. Hodge
258 Jan. 6 Tor. Bower
259 Jan. 9 Det. Crozier
260 Jan. 9 Det. Crozier
261 Jan. 16 N.Y. Plante
262 Jan. 20 Bos. Johnston
263 Feb. 6 Det. Sawchuk
264 Mar. 20 Mon. Hodge

### 1965–66
265 Oct. 23 Tor. Bower
266 Oct. 23 Tor. Bower
267 Oct. 23 Tor. Bower
268 Oct. 24 Bos. Johnston
269 Oct. 28 Det. Crozier
270 Oct. 28 Det. Crozier
271 Oct. 30 Mon. Worsley
272 Oct. 30 Mon. Hodge
273 Nov. 7 Tor. Sawchuk
274 Nov. 7 Tor. Sawchuk
275 Nov. 7 Tor. Sawchuk
276 Nov. 13 Mon. Worsley
277 Nov. 17 N.Y. Giacomin
278 Nov. 17 N.Y. Giacomin
279 Nov. 20 Tor. Sawchuk
280 Dec. 4 Bos. Parent
281 Dec. 5 N.Y. Giacomin
282 Dec. 15 Bos. Cheevers
283 Dec. 15 Bos. Cheevers
284 Dec. 15 Bos. Cheevers
285 Dec. 15 Bos. Cheevers
286 Dec. 19 Det. Crozier
287 Dec. 19 Det. Crozier
288 Dec. 22 N.Y. Simmons
289 Dec. 22 N.Y. Simmons
290 Dec. 25 Tor. Sawchuk
291 Dec. 25 Tor. Sawchuk
292 Dec. 31 Det. Crozier
293 Jan. 2 Bos. Johnston

| 294 | JAN. 5 | MON. | WORSLEY |
| 295 | JAN. 5 | MON. | WORSLEY |
| 296 | JAN. 9 | TOR. | SAWCHUK |
| 297 | JAN. 16 | N.Y. | MANIAGO |
| 298 | JAN. 16 | N.Y. | MANIAGO |
| 299 | JAN. 16 | N.Y. | MANIAGO |
| 300 | JAN. 16 | N.Y. | MANIAGO |
| 301 | JAN. 20 | BOS. | JOHNSTON |
| 302 | JAN. 23 | MON. | WORSLEY |
| 303 | JAN. 26 | MON. | HODGE |
| 304 | JAN. 27 | BOS. | JOHNSTON |
| 305 | JAN. 29 | DET. | CROZIER |
| 306 | JAN. 29 | DET. | CROZIER |
| 307 | FEB. 2 | N.Y. | GIACOMIN |
| 308 | FEB. 2 | N.Y. | GIACOMIN |
| 309 | FEB. 12 | MON. | WORSLEY |
| 310 | FEB. 16 | N.Y. | GIACOMIN |
| 311 | FEB. 20 | BOS. | JOHNSTON |
| 312 | FEB. 26 | DET. | CROZIER |
| 313 | FEB. 27 | BOS. | PARENT |
| 314 | MAR. 2 | DET. | BASSEN |
| 315 | MAR. 12 | N.Y. | MANIAGO |
| 316 | MAR. 13 | TOR. | GAMBLE |
| 317 | MAR. 16 | DET. | CROZIER |
| 318 | APR. 2 | MON. | WORSLEY |

## 1966–67

| 319 | OCT. 19 | N.Y. | GIACOMIN |
| 320 | OCT. 19 | N.Y. | GIACOMIN |
| 321 | OCT. 22 | DET. | CROZIER |
| 322 | OCT. 26 | MON. | WORSLEY |
| 323 | NOV. 13 | TOR. | GAMBLE |
| 324 | NOV. 13 | TOR. | GAMBLE |
| 325 | NOV. 16 | N.Y. | GIACOMIN |
| 326 | NOV. 19 | DET. | CROZIER |
| 327 | NOV. 19 | DET. | CROZIER |
| 328 | DEC. 8 | BOS. | CHEEVERS |
| 329 | DEC. 17 | MON. | HODGE |
| 330 | DEC. 21 | DET. | CROZIER |
| 331 | DEC. 21 | DET. | CROZIER |
| 332 | DEC. 27 | N.Y. | GIACOMIN |
| 333 | DEC. 31 | TOR. | A. SMITH |
| 334 | JAN. 4 | MON. | HODGE |
| 335 | JAN. 4 | MON. | HODGE |
| 336 | JAN. 5 | DET. | CROZIER |
| 337 | JAN. 5 | DET. | CROZIER |
| 338 | JAN. 11 | DET. | CROZIER |
| 339 | JAN. 11 | DET. | CROZIER |
| 340 | JAN. 11 | DET. | CROZIER |
| 341 | JAN. 12 | DET. | CROZIER |
| 342 | JAN. 14 | N.Y. | GIACOMIN |
| 343 | JAN. 15 | TOR. | GAMBLE |
| 344 | JAN. 15 | TOR. | GAMBLE |
| 345 | JAN. 21 | MON. | HODGE |
| 346 | JAN. 21 | MON. | HODGE |
| 347 | JAN. 26 | DET. | CROZIER |
| 348 | JAN. 26 | DET. | CROZIER |
| 349 | FEB. 1 | BOS. | PARENT |
| 350 | FEB. 6 | BOS. | JOHNSTON |
| 351 | FEB. 8 | MON. | WORSLEY |
| 352 | FEB. 8 | MON. | WORSLEY |
| 353 | FEB. 11 | TOR. | GAMBLE |
| 354 | FEB. 11 | TOR. | GAMBLE |
| 355 | FEB. 11 | TOR. | GAMBLE |
| 356 | FEB. 19 | N.Y. | GIACOMIN |
| 357 | FEB. 25 | BOS. | PARENT |
| 358 | FEB. 25 | BOS. | PARENT |
| 359 | MAR. 1 | N.Y. | GIACOMIN |
| 360 | MAR. 1 | N.Y. | GIACOMIN |
| 361 | MAR. 1 | N.Y. | GIACOMIN |
| 362 | MAR. 2 | BOS. | JOHNSTON |
| 363 | MAR. 5 | TOR. | BOWER |
| 364 | MAR. 5 | TOR. | BOWER |
| 365 | MAR. 8 | BOS. | PARENT |
| 366 | MAR. 12 | TOR. | SAWCHUK |
| 367 | MAR. 15 | N.Y. | GIACOMIN |
| 368 | MAR. 18 | TOR. | GAMBLE |
| 369 | MAR. 19 | MON. | VACHON |
| 370 | MAR. 22 | N.Y. | GIACOMIN |

## 1967–68

| 371 | OCT. 11 | N.Y. | GIACOMIN |
| 372 | OCT. 11 | N.Y. | GIACOMIN |
| 373 | OCT. 15 | TOR. | BOWER |
| 374 | OCT. 18 | BOS. | CHEEVERS |
| 375 | OCT. 21 | PITTS. | BINKLEY |
| 376 | OCT. 22 | L.A. | SAWCHUK |
| 377 | OCT. 25 | N.Y. | GIACOMIN |
| 378 | OCT. 28 | MINN. | MANIAGO |
| 379 | OCT. 28 | MINN. | BAUMAN |
| 380 | NOV. 2 | L.A. | SAWCHUK |
| 381 | NOV. 5 | OAK. | HODGE |
| 382 | NOV. 11 | MON. | VACHON |
| 383 | NOV. 12 | ST.L. | G. HALL |
| 384 | NOV. 12 | ST.L. | G. HALL |
| 385 | NOV. 15 | ST.L. | G. HALL |
| 386 | NOV. 22 | N.Y. | GIACOMIN |
| 387 | NOV. 22 | N.Y. | GIACOMIN |
| 388 | NOV. 22 | N.Y. | GIACOMIN |
| 389 | NOV. 29 | PHIL. | PARENT |
| 390 | DEC. 6 | PITTS. | BASSEN |
| 391 | DEC. 6 | PITTS. | BASSEN |
| 392 | DEC. 9 | MON. | WORSLEY |
| 393 | DEC. 10 | PHIL. | FAVELL |
| 394 | DEC. 10 | PHIL. | FAVELL |
| 395 | DEC. 13 | N.Y. | GIACOMIN |
| 396 | DEC. 20 | BOS. | CHEEVERS |
| 397 | DEC. 20 | BOS. | CHEEVERS |
| 398 | DEC. 30 | N.Y. | SIMMONS |
| 399 | JAN. 6 | DET. | EDWARDS |
| 400 | JAN. 7 | BOS. | CHEEVERS |
| 401 | JAN. 7 | BOS. | CHEEVERS |
| 402 | JAN. 13 | DET. | GARDNER |
| 403 | JAN. 27 | TOR. | GAMBLE |
| 404 | JAN. 27 | TOR. | GAMBLE |
| 405 | JAN. 31 | N.Y. | SIMMONS |
| 406 | FEB. 4 | L.A. | RUTLEDGE |
| 407 | FEB. 7 | TOR. | BOWER |
| 408 | FEB. 10 | MON. | WORSLEY |
| 409 | FEB. 14 | BOS. | CHEEVERS |
| 410 | FEB. 18 | DET. | CROZIER |
| 411 | FEB. 21 | OAK. | HODGE |
| 412 | MAR. 2 | ST.L. | G. HALL |
| 413 | MAR. 13 | PITTS. | BASSEN |
| 414 | MAR. 17 | OAK. | G. SMITH |

## 1968–69

| 415 | OCT. 13 | N.Y. | GIACOMIN |
| 416 | OCT. 16 | MINN. | RIVARD |
| 417 | OCT. 19 | TOR. | A. SMITH |
| 418 | OCT. 23 | PITTS. | BINKLEY |
| 419 | OCT. 23 | PITTS. | BINKLEY |
| 420 | OCT. 27 | DET. | CROZIER |
| 421 | OCT. 30 | L.A. | RUTLEDGE |
| 422 | NOV. 1 | OAK. | G. SMITH |
| 423 | NOV. 3 | BOS. | CHEEVERS |
| 424 | NOV. 13 | PITTS. | DALEY |
| 425 | NOV. 14 | PITTS. | BINKLEY |
| 426 | NOV. 14 | PITTS. | BINKLEY |
| 427 | NOV. 14 | PITTS. | BINKLEY |
| 428 | NOV. 17 | TOR. | GAMBLE |
| 429 | NOV. 21 | N.Y. | GIACOMIN |
| 430 | DEC. 1 | MON. | VACHON |
| 431 | DEC. 8 | BOS. | CHEEVERS |
| 432 | DEC. 8 | BOS. | CHEEVERS |
| 433 | DEC. 8 | BOS. | CHEEVERS |
| 434 | DEC. 11 | ST.L. | G. HALL |
| 435 | DEC. 14 | BOS. | CHEEVERS |
| 436 | DEC. 22 | PITTS. | BINKLEY |
| 437 | DEC. 29 | L.A. | DESJARDINS |
| 438 | JAN. 1 | DET. | EDWARDS |
| 439 | JAN. 2 | PHIL. | FAVELL |
| 440 | JAN. 4 | MON. | WORSLEY |
| 441 | JAN. 4 | MON. | WORSLEY |
| 442 | JAN. 8 | ST.L. | PLANTE |
| 443 | JAN. 12 | L.A. | DESJARDINS |
| 444 | JAN. 12 | L.A. | DESJARDINS |
| 445 | JAN. 26 | L.A. | DESJARDINS |
| 446 | FEB. 1 | MINN. | MANIAGO |
| 447 | FEB. 8 | DET. | EDWARDS |
| 448 | FEB. 9 | TOR. | GAMBLE |
| 449 | FEB. 11 | BOS. | JOHNSTON |
| 450 | FEB. 12 | PHIL. | PARENT |
| 451 | FEB. 16 | BOS. | JOHNSTON |
| 452 | FEB. 19 | OAK. | G. SMITH |
| 453 | FEB. 20 | L.A. | CARON |
| 454 | FEB. 20 | L.A. | CARON |
| 455 | FEB. 20 | L.A. | CARON |
| 456 | FEB. 22 | TOR. | GAMBLE |
| 457 | FEB. 26 | N.Y. | GIACOMIN |
| 458 | FEB. 27 | PITTS. | DALEY |
| 459 | FEB. 27 | PITTS. | DALEY |
| 460 | MAR. 2 | TOR. | GAMBLE |
| 461 | MAR. 3 | MINN. | RIVARD |
| 462 | MAR. 3 | MINN. | RIVARD |
| 463 | MAR. 5 | N.Y. | GIACOMIN |
| 464 | MAR. 5 | N.Y. | GIACOMIN |
| 465 | MAR. 12 | OAK. | G. SMITH |
| 466 | MAR. 16 | PHIL. | PARENT |
| 467 | MAR. 16 | PHIL. | PARENT |
| 468 | MAR. 20 | BOS. | CHEEVERS |
| 469 | MAR. 20 | BOS. | CHEEVERS |
| 470 | MAR. 26 | N.Y. | GIACOMIN |
| 471 | MAR. 29 | DET. | EDWARDS |
| 472 | MAR. 30 | DET. | CROZIER |

## 1969–70

| 473 | NOV. 23 | PITTS. | A. SMITH |
| 474 | NOV. 26 | L.A. | DESJARDINS |
| 475 | NOV. 29 | DET. | EDWARDS |
| 476 | NOV. 30 | ST.L. | WAKELY |
| 477 | DEC. 3 | N.Y. | GIACOMIN |
| 478 | DEC. 7 | DET. | EDWARDS |
| 479 | DEC. 14 | PHIL. | FAVELL |
| 480 | DEC. 19 | OAK. | G. SMITH |
| 481 | DEC. 25 | MINN. | RIVARD |
| 482 | DEC. 27 | PITTS. | BINKLEY |
| 483 | JAN. 7 | DET. | EDWARDS |
| 484 | JAN. 10 | ST.L. | PLANTE |
| 485 | JAN. 14 | PITTS. | A. SMITH |
| 486 | JAN. 22 | DET. | EDWARDS |
| 487 | JAN. 24 | MON. | VACHON |
| 488 | JAN. 25 | TOR. | GAMBLE |
| 489 | JAN. 31 | PHIL. | FAVELL |
| 490 | JAN. 31 | PHIL. | FAVELL |
| 491 | FEB. 4 | BOS. | JOHNSTON |
| 492 | FEB. 1 | BOS. | JOHNSTON |
| 493 | FEB. 7 | PHIL. | FAVELL |
| 494 | FEB. 11 | PITTS. | A. SMITH |
| 495 | FEB. 11 | PITTS. | A. SMITH |
| 496 | FEB. 15 | TOR. | GAMBLE |
| 497 | FEB. 15 | TOR. | GAMBLE |
| 498 | FEB. 19 | MINN. | MANIAGO |
| 499 | FEB. 21 | N.Y. | GIACOMIN |
| 500 | FEB. 21 | N.Y. | GIACOMIN |
| 501 | FEB. 22 | BOS. | CHEEVERS |
| 502 | FEB. 26 | PHIL. | WILSON |
| 503 | FEB. 26 | PHIL. | WILSON |
| 504 | MAR. 14 | N.Y. | SAWCHUK |
| 505 | MAR. 18 | TOR. | GAMBLE |
| 506 | MAR. 18 | TOR. | GAMBLE |
| 507 | MAR. 29 | TOR. | M. EDWARDS |
| 508 | MAR. 29 | TOR. | M. EDWARDS |
| 509 | APR. 5 | MON. | VACHON |
| 510 | APR. 5 | MON. | VACHON |

## 1970–71

| 511 | OCT. 11 | OAK. | SNEDDON |
| 512 | OCT. 14 | VAN. | GARDNER |
| 513 | OCT. 15 | DET. | R. EDWARDS |
| 514 | OCT. 31 | PITTS. | A. SMITH |
| 515 | NOV. 8 | MINN. | GILBERT |
| 516 | NOV. 11 | PHIL. | PARENT |
| 517 | NOV. 11 | PHIL. | PARENT |
| 518 | NOV. 14 | N.Y. | VILLEMURE |
| 519 | NOV. 22 | OAK. | SNEDDON |
| 520 | NOV. 22 | OAK. | SNEDDON |
| 521 | NOV. 22 | OAK. | SNEDDON |
| 522 | NOV. 25 | MON. | VACHON |
| 523 | DEC. 6 | TOR. | GAMBLE |
| 524 | DEC. 12 | TOR. | PLANTE |
| 525 | DEC. 16 | ST.L. | WAKELY |
| 526 | DEC. 20 | PITTS. | A. SMITH |
| 527 | DEC. 22 | OAK. | G. SMITH |
| 528 | DEC. 23 | L.A. | DEJORDY |
| 529 | DEC. 23 | L.A. | DEJORDY |
| 530 | DEC. 31 | DET. | MCLEOD |
| 531 | JAN. 2 | PHIL. | PARENT |
| 532 | JAN. 3 | BUFF. | DALEY |
| 533 | JAN. 3 | BUFF. | DALEY |
| 534 | JAN. 9 | BOS. | CHEEVERS |
| 535 | JAN. 17 | N.Y. | VILLEMURE |
| 536 | JAN. 21 | DET. | RUTHERFORD |
| 537 | JAN. 24 | OAK. | G. SMITH |
| 538 | JAN. 24 | OAK. | G. SMITH |
| 539 | JAN. 26 | VAN. | HODGE |
| 540 | FEB. 3 | N.Y. | GIACOMIN |
| 541 | FEB. 6 | MINN. | GILBERT |
| 542 | FEB. 6 | MINN. | GILBERT |
| 543 | FEB. 6 | MINN. | GILBERT |
| 544 | FEB. 7 | PITTS. | BINKLEY |
| 545 | FEB. 14 | VAN. | HODGE |
| 546 | FEB. 14 | VAN. | HODGE |
| 547 | FEB. 21 | L.A. | DEJORDY |
| 548 | FEB. 21 | L.A. | DEJORDY |
| 549 | FEB. 21 | L.A. | DEJORDY |
| 550 | MAR. 3 | ST.L. | WAKELY |
| 551 | MAR. 16 | VAN. | GARDNER |
| 552 | MAR. 19 | OAK. | G. SMITH |
| 553 | MAR. 21 | DET. | GRAY |
| 554 | MAR. 24 | BOS. | CHEEVERS |

## 1971–72

| 555 | OCT. 9 | ST.L. | WAKELY |
| 556 | OCT. 9 | ST.L. | WAKELY |
| 557 | OCT. 16 | MINN. | MANIAGO |
| 558 | OCT. 21 | BUFF. | CROZIER |
| 559 | OCT. 26 | DET. | DALEY |
| 560 | NOV. 7 | PITTS. | R. EDWARDS |
| 561 | NOV. 10 | BOS. | CHEEVERS |
| 562 | NOV. 14 | CALIF. | MELOCHE |
| 563 | NOV. 20 | BOS. | CHEEVERS |
| 564 | NOV. 21 | PITTS. | RUTHERFORD |
| 565 | NOV. 27 | TOR. | PARENT |
| 566 | NOV. 28 | TOR. | PARENT |
| 567 | DEC. 5 | L.A. | VACHON |
| 568 | DEC. 5 | L.A. | EDWARDS |
| 569 | DEC. 8 | N.Y. | GIACOMIN |
| 570 | DEC. 11 | TOR. | PLANTE |
| 571 | DEC. 12 | MINN. | WORSLEY |
| 572 | DEC. 15 | BUFF. | DRYDEN |
| 573 | DEC. 15 | BUFF. | DRYDEN |
| 574 | DEC. 18 | MINN. | MANIAGO |
| 575 | DEC. 19 | ST.L. | WAKELY |
| 576 | DEC. 22 | CALIF. | MELOCHE |
| 577 | DEC. 22 | CALIF. | MELOCHE |
| 578 | DEC. 22 | CALIF. | MELOCHE |
| 579 | DEC. 26 | L.A. | VACHON |
| 580 | JAN. 2 | PHIL. | FAVELL |
| 581 | JAN. 2 | PHIL. | GAMBLE |
| 582 | JAN. 5 | PITTS. | RUTHERFORD |
| 583 | JAN. 12 | N.Y. | GIACOMIN |
| 584 | JAN. 15 | BOS. | CHEEVERS |
| 585 | JAN. 16 | MINN. | MANIAGO |
| 586 | JAN. 19 | CALIF. | MELOCHE |
| 587 | JAN. 19 | CALIF. | MELOCHE |
| 588 | JAN. 20 | PHIL. | GAMBLE |
| 589 | JAN. 23 | TOR. | PARENT |
| 590 | JAN. 30 | DET. | A. SMITH |
| 591 | FEB. 4 | VAN. | WILSON |
| 592 | FEB. 9 | N.Y. | GIACOMIN |
| 593 | FEB. 12 | DET. | A. SMITH |
| 594 | FEB. 26 | CALIF. | MELOCHE |
| 595 | MAR. 1 | L.A. | B. SMITH |
| 596 | MAR. 3 | CALIF. | MELOCHE |
| 597 | MAR. 8 | N.Y. | GIACOMIN |
| 598 | MAR. 18 | TOR. | PLANTE |
| 599 | MAR. 23 | PHIL. | MCLEOD |
| 600 | MAR. 25 | BOS. | CHEEVERS |
| 601 | MAR. 26 | ST.L. | WAKELY |
| 602 | APR. 1 | ST.L. | CARON |
| 603 | APR. 2 | DET. | BROWN |
| 604 | APR. 2 | DET. | BROWN |

THIS IS IN 1968, at the annual Christmas party staged by the Blackhawks at the Chicago Stadium. Management was always good about that, no matter where we were in the standings. From left are Bobby, Blake, Brett, and their mother. First time on skates for Brett.

# CHAPTER FOUR

# A Hockey Family

HOCKEY AND *HULL* ARE SYN-ONYMS. Shortly after Bobby scored two goals in a 1957 exhibition game against the New York Rangers, he called home to his father, Robert Sr., who had been a pretty fair player in his day. "Can you come here?" Bobby asked from St. Catharines, Ontario, three hours away. Mom thought something was amiss, but no, Bobby told her that he was being asked to turn pro in training camp with the Blackhawks for the princely sum of $6,500. "We don't have that kind of money!" shouted Dad. But Robert Sr., who had imparted much of his knowledge and energy toward his son, soon grasped the magnitude of the situation. Bobby was headed toward the NHL.

Similarly, as if to pass the baton, Bobby would later mentor his son Brett. "When I was in Winnipeg, my wife and I split," recalls Bobby. "Brett went with her to Vancouver. A few years later, in 1982, I was there for *Hockey Night in Canada*, doing analysis for the Stanley Cup Finals. I saw Brett and told him to get with it. You see, those years in Winnipeg, he got used to going to the rink with me. When I wasn't there anymore, when he really needed a father, he didn't have me to go the rink with. So he kind of drifted off. Whatever I told him, it must have had an effect."

Indeed, like his father, Brett went on to enjoy a fabulous career, eventually joining his dad in hockey's Hall of Fame. Bobby's other sons were athletes, too. Bobby Jr. won the Memorial Cup with Cornwall, Blake the Allan Cup with Brantford. Bart was a star running back in college, then the Canadian Football League. "All three were pretty good hockey players," said Bobby. "Blake, on any given night, was as nice a player as you would ever see. Bobby could put the biscuit in the basket. They all did fine outside hockey. Brett was the one who was least bothered by having the name 'Hull.' It just rolled off his back, and once he put his mind to it, well, the record speaks for itself. I will tell you that no one got more done with less work. Brett was so smart, such a student of the game. Look at what he did after he retired. He became an executive. He had the physical and mental attributes to come into his own. I always said my Chicago teammate, Stan Mikita, was the best player ever, pound for pound. But Brett, I might have to give him the nod now."

Not to be forgotten is Bobby's brother Dennis, also a prolific left winger for the Blackhawks. Dennis, however, recognized the inevitable comparisons to Bobby, then Brett, and even wrote a book about it titled *The Third Best Hull* ("I would have been fourth but they wouldn't let my sister Maxine play," he joked). ■

HERE I AM WITH BRETT, who was born in the summer of 1964, my third son. Years later, Brett made his NHL debut with the Calgary Flames. The coach there, Terry Crisp, was of the opinion that Brett wouldn't amount to much, which tells you all you need to know about Crisp's eye for talent.

THIS IS BRETT AND ME AGAIN. I am reading him a book. I don't know for sure what the book was about. Maybe it was a book on how to score goals. If it was, Brett must have absorbed whatever was in it, because by the end of his career, he could have written a book on the subject.

BOBBY IS TRYING ON AN AUTHENTIC BLACKHAWKS JERSEY, maybe for the first time. Brett could have worn it for real, but their general manager, Bob Pulford, passed on chances to draft him, then trade for him. Pulford said Brett was "too slow." Pulford must have done his scouting from Brett's baby pictures.

DURING SOME SPARE TIME IN OUR LOCKER ROOM, Bobby (left) and Blake take a look at some snapshots of me in game action. It was not uncommon when I was with the Blackhawks for players to bring their kids to the office, which for us was the Stadium. It was great to have them hanging out with us.

# 913

## TOTAL NHL GOALS SCORED BY BROTHERS BOBBY AND DENNIS HULL.

BOBBY (LEFT) AND BLAKE WITH THEIR MOTHER AND ME ARE IN POINT ANNE, ONTARIO, during the summer. As you can see, we're standing by this huge sign, I want to say it was 20 feet by 12 feet, informing everybody that Point Anne was the birthplace of yours truly. The population of our town was pretty small. There weren't many people who lived there, but there were a whole lot of Hulls. Every summer, brother Dennis would write in that he, too, was born here. Then, every year after we left to go back to playing hockey, Dennis' name was erased.

BOBBY JR., YOURS TRULY, AND BLAKE SPORTING UNIFORMS OF THE MOTT'S CLAMATOS, a Senior A team in the Ontario Hockey Association based in Brantford, Ontario. With Blake playing for them, the Clamatos won the Allan Cup in 1986–87.

HERE WE ARE AGAIN, the three amigos. Bobby and Blake and me. It's bedtime for them at our summer home on the Bay of Quinte. I didn't get that tan from winters in Chicago.

BOBBY (LEFT) AND BLAKE ARE WITH THEIR MOTHER AFTER I SCORED MY 51ST GOAL OF THE SEASON ON MARCH 12, 1966, at the Stadium against Cesare Maniago of the New York Rangers. Rocket Richard and Bernie "Boom Boom" Geoffrion were the only other players who had reached 50 at that time.

I AM ACTING AS A LINESMAN, dropping the puck for a ceremonial face-off between Bobby and Blake, who are dressed to the nines in their Blackhawks gear. Both of them went on to play junior and senior hockey, but never made it to the pros.

BLAKE (LEFT), BOBBY, AND BRETT ARE WORKING ON A MILK SHAKE. Normally, the boys would be excited by the prospect, but maybe they were feeling bad for Dad. I had a broken jaw after an encounter with Ron Harris of the Red Wings in December of 1968 and was on a milk shake diet myself.

BOBBY JR. IS WITH YOURS TRULY AND DENNIS in 1965, my brother's rookie year with the Blackhawks.

THIS IS A MUCH HAPPIER OCCASION, as you can tell by my smile. Bobby and Brett are there to help me celebrate my 500th NHL goal, scored against Ed Giacomin of the New York Rangers on February 21, 1970. Three pucks, tape, and a felt-tip pen made my makeshift trophy.

# 1987 THE YEAR BOBBY'S SON BLAKE WON THE ALLAN CUP, PLAYING ON THE BRANTFORD MOTT'S CLAMATOS OF THE OHA SENIOR A HOCKEY LEAGUE.

ANOTHER CHRISTMAS PARTY AT THE STADIUM WITH BLAKE, BRETT, AND BOBBY, ALONG WITH THEIR MOTHER. I don't know if this is before or after we all got to meet Santa Claus, but I do know that the owners and management did a nice job of making it feel special. There were always gifts for the kids and the players, maybe TV sets or plane tickets. I had my moments with the front office, but I have to say we were treated well on Christmas. One thing I noticed about the current Blackhawks: a lot of them are young and single. Not as many children running around, but who can argue with the 2010 Stanley Cup?

DENNIS AND I ARE AT A CATTLE SHOW in Chicago's International Amphitheatre in 1965 with one of our prized possessions, Oakland Ridge Lamp. One of my favorite pastimes. I still am in the business to this day.

THE BOYS ARE GROW-
ING BEFORE MY EYES
AND DRESSING UP IN
FANCIER CLOTHES, TOO.
Well, maybe not Brett, who is
in the middle between Bobby
(left) and Blake. On the
right is Tommy Ivan, general
manager of the Blackhawks.
Years later, during the winter of 1972, I was called to
a meeting with Arthur and
Bill Wirtz, the team own-
ers, and Ivan. I was asked if I
was happy in Chicago. That
was when the World Hockey
Association started making
noise. The Blackhawks never
thought I would leave. Nei-
ther did I. But I did.

BOBBY (LEFT) AND BRETT ARE WITH COACH BILLY REAY AFTER I SCORED MY 604TH REGULAR-SEASON GOAL FOR THE BLACKHAWKS ON APRIL 2, 1972. As I mentioned, things were beginning to heat up at that point and, as it turned out, that was my last goal for the Blackhawks. Soon I was off to Winnipeg.

MY MOTHER LENA WAS A GREAT SUPPORTER OF US KIDS, and there were 11 of us. Here we are at the 1971 NHL All-Star Game, and Mom planted a big smooch on me.

DAD AND I CELEBRATE after I won the Lester Patrick Trophy in 1969 for contributions to hockey in the United States. It is named after a longtime executive of the New York Rangers.

BROTHER DENNIS AND I RETURN THE AFFECTION
WITH MOM, again at the 1971 All-Star Game. Dennis and I
had more hair then than we do now. Dennis has a great sense
of humor, often making fun of himself, but he was an excellent
player, despite what he says.

Over her features poured a ray
Of glory never to pass away,
Her eleven children she loved alone
The greatest love we've ever known.

Years over her snowy head have passed
But children came, Laura first and Peggy last,
Never, ever to be alone on earth
Of grandchildren she has no dearth.

Her children—she made us all aspire
To do our best with flair and fire,
Her oldest son known both near and far
But she thinks each of us is a star.

Thanks, thanks our worthy Mother
We love you dearly all sisters and brothers,
Your grandchildren who live in every place
They also love your sweet embrace.

So many words, so much ado
But you were always strong and true,
We get together so very few days
I only came to sing your praise.

*A poem my brother Dennis wrote for our mother
on her 80th birthday.*

A FAMILY PHOTO WITH DAD, who is seated. From left: Peggy, Judy, Dennis, Gary, Ron, yours truly, Laura, Barbara,
Jacqueline, Maxine, and Caroline. The queen, mother Lena Marguerite, is not in the picture, but she's in our hearts.

I LACED THEM UP WITH BRETT FOR A CHARITY GAME WHEN HE WAS AT THE
UNIVERSITY OF MINNESOTA–DULUTH, which he attended during the mid-1980s. I was on the
ice with him for 20 seconds when I realized he could play with any team, in any league, in any era.

WHEN I WAS PLAYING AND THE KIDS
WERE STILL YOUNG, I WAS OFTEN
ASKED WHICH OF MY SONS I THOUGHT
COULD MAKE IT BIG IN THE NHL. I
always pointed to the pudgy one, Brett. "If
he ever gets a fire in his belly," I kept telling
people, "he will be something special." Well,
Brett got the fire in his belly, and here he is with
that Hart Trophy again, an award I was fortunate enough to win in 1965 and 1966. In 1991,
the runner-up to Brett was Wayne Gretzky, who
won eight straight of them in the 1980s.

# O

OTHER THAN BOBBY AND BRETT, THE NUMBER OF FATHER-SON TANDEMS TO EACH HAVE THEIR NUMBER RETIRED.

THIS IS "THE GOLDEN BRETT" AFTER HE SCORED HIS 611TH GOAL IN THE NHL, surpassing my mark of 610 that included six I had with the Winnipeg Jets and Hartford Whalers after they moved over from the WHA. At the time, Brett was with the Dallas Stars, with whom he signed as a free agent before the 1998–99 season after playing 11 years with the Blues. Brett scored his 600th and 601st goals with Dallas on New Year's Eve 1999, and went on to win the Stanley Cup with the Stars. Amazing to think that back in the day, Dallas was a farm club of the Blackhawks.

WHEN BRETT WAS TEARING IT UP WITH THE BLUES, he had a restaurant in St. Louis. He and I are in the front. From left in the back are Bobby, Bart, and Blake. The restaurant business is a tough one, but when you score 70 goals a year like Brett did, you own the town.

MY HALL OF FAME INDUCTION IN TORONTO IN 1983. From left are Stan Mikita, Harry Sinden, NHL president John Ziegler, yours truly, and Ken Dryden. Stan and I getting in on the same night was terrific. Harry was a longtime general manager and coach with the Boston Bruins. Ken Dryden was the Montreal Canadiens goalie who killed us in the 1971 Stanley Cup Finals.

MY INDUCTION SPEECH at the Hall of Fame.

HERE'S BRETT WITH HIS CUP IN DALLAS after the Stars beat the Buffalo Sabres in the finals. He scored the winner in Game 6 on his own rebound in the third overtime.

BRETT WASN'T DONE YET. He signed with Detroit, and in 2002 he won another Cup with the Red Wings. He had 30 goals for them, on his way to a career total of 741.

IN DECEMBER 2006, the Blues retired Brett's No. 16. I was at the ceremony, but Brett didn't know about it until I walked out to center ice. Very emotional.

BRETT IS IN A JACKET AND TIE here because he is retired and now a member of the Dallas Stars' front office. A co–general manager. I knew he would make it big. With him at the United Center are yours truly and two dear friends, Dr. Jeff Lapsker and Jim Pender.

# 1,351 TOTAL NHL GOALS SCORED BY BOBBY AND BRETT HULL.

**WHEN BRETT JOINED THE PHOENIX COYOTES,** they unretired No. 9 so he could wear it. The No. 9 had been retired when I played for the Winnipeg Jets, who moved to Phoenix and became the Coyotes.

MY DAUGHTER-IN-LAW DARCIE, SON BRETT, AND WIFE DEBORAH pose with yours truly on the night Brett was inducted into the Hockey Hall of Fame.

MY FRIENDS Jay McGreevy, Mayor Richard M. Daley, and football legends Paul Hornung and Dick Butkus.

PAUL HORNUNG AGAIN, an all-time great with Notre Dame and the Green Bay Packers.

KEN NORTON, a famous heavyweight boxer who beat Muhammad Ali in 1973 and broke Ali's jaw in the process.

ED LITZENBERGER, STAN MIKITA, YOURS TRULY, AND AL VIOLA are having a good time, probably reciting one of our favorite poems: "The horse and mule live 30 years and never knows of wines and beers. The goat and sheep at 20 die without a taste of scotch or rye. The cow drinks water by the ton and at 18 is mostly done. The dog at 15 cashes in without the aid of rum or gin. The modest, sober, bone-dry hen lays eggs for noggs and dies at 10. But sinful, ginful, rum-soaked men survive three-score years and 10. And some of us though mighty few stay pickled 'til we're 92."

DOUG BUFFONE, A CHICAGO BEARS LINEBACKER from 1966 through 1979, and a fun guy to be around.

STEVE CARLTON, Hall of Fame left-hander who starred for the St. Louis Cardinals and Philadelphia Phillies. He won four Cy Young Awards and 329 games.

JIM PENDER, my good friend, wearing my No. 9.

MUHAMMAD ALI, aka Cassius Clay. Maybe the greatest heavyweight boxer ever.

BEFORE THE BLACKHAWKS' 2009–10 REGULAR-SEASON HOME OPENER, I went on the ice. I don't remember the last time I was on skates before that night, and once I got going, I needed help to stop or I would have just kept going.

# CHAPTER FIVE

# Coming Home

I N THE SPRING OF 1972, after breaking all the Blackhawks' scoring records throughout his 15-year career, Bobby Hull signed a long-term contract with the Winnipeg Jets of the World Hockey Association, a rival league that needed a star player. Hull's departure sent shock waves throughout Chicago, where he remains one of the most popular athletes ever. Upon leaving, the Golden Jet and the franchise he helped make famous endured decades of detachment. But that changed when Rocky Wirtz took over as chairman of the Blackhawks from his deceased father, Bill, in 2007 and promptly hired John McDonough as president.

"One of the first phone calls I made was to Bobby," said McDonough. "I wanted him to know that we were out of the grudge business and would love to have him back as part of our organization. We were on the phone for about two hours, and most of the conversation was one-way, if you know what I mean. I put my listening skills to good use."

Hull was surprised by the gesture, and not initially convinced. But after subsequent discussions with Wirtz and McDonough, the Golden Jet agreed to become a team ambassador, joining a list that soon would include fellow Hall of Famers Stan Mikita, Tony Esposito, and Denis Savard.

"I had said some things over the years that weren't too kind to the Blackhawks, but Rocky and John wanted to hear me out, and they did," said Hull, who immediately became a fixture at home games, including the regular-season opener at the United Center when the four ambassadors suited up and skated onto the ice. "It was a secret, and it was an unbelievable night," said Hull. "But it was in keeping with how Rocky and John have built a whole new feeling about the Blackhawks. The four of us do whatever is asked, whether it's signing autographs or making appearances, anything to promote hockey in this great city. Leaving the Blackhawks was the worst mistake I ever made, and I never thought that I would be back with the only franchise I had known from 1957 until I left. A lot of bridges were burned, but as John said, 'If you're at war with your past, it's difficult to build a future.' I felt a tremendous void without the Blackhawks, and Rocky and John will never know what this has meant to my family and me. It's wonderful to be back. That phone call changed my life." ∎

BOBBY'S #9 JERSEY WAS RETIRED BY THE CHICAGO BLACKHAWKS ON **DECEMBER 18, 1983.**

ON DECEMBER 18, 1983, SHORTLY AFTER MY HALL OF FAME INDUCTION, the Blackhawks retired my No. 9 jersey. I am at the ceremony in the Stadium with team owner Bill Wirtz.

I WALK OUT ON THE STADIUM ICE for the last time in April 1994 before the Blackhawks moved across the street to the United Center.

WE HAD A PREGAME CEREMONY for the final regular-season game at the Stadium, and here I am shaking hands with Bill Wirtz, owner of the Blackhawks. On the left smiling is Tommy Ivan, who was the team's longtime general manager and a tough man when it came to talking contracts.

I'M IN PRETTY GOOD COMPANY HERE. To my left are Jean Beliveau, the great former captain of the Montreal Canadiens; Gordie Howe and his Detroit Red Wings' jersey; and Maurice "Rocket" Richard, another legend with Les Canadiens.

I RECEIVED A LIFETIME ACHIEVEMENT AWARD IN 2009 FROM COM-CAST, presented by Jim Corno (left) of the network that televises Blackhawks games and other sports in Chicago. On the right is John McDonough, the Blackhawks' president who made the phone call that brought me back.

MORE GOOD COMPANY. From left: Tony Esposito, Pierre Pilote, yours truly, Denis Savard, and Stan Mikita. Tony, Denis, and Stan are fellow ambassadors. Pierre, another Hall of Famer, was a great defenseman.

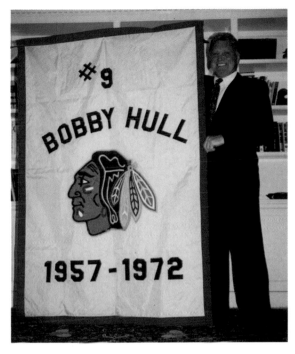

THIS IS THE BANNER MARKING THE YEARS I WAS WITH THE BLACKHAWKS, all at the great old barn, the Chicago Stadium. Fans would line up outside, then run in when the doors opened and climb up to the second balcony for standing-room-only tickets. The banner and I are in my living room.

THIS IS AT A GOLF OUTING HOSTED BY CHRIS CHELIOS AND JEREMY ROENICK, two guys who were stars with the Blackhawks long after I left. My cigar and I are standing with Gordie Howe, one of the greatest players I ever played against. He was a right wing with the Detroit Red Wings, I was a left wing with the Blackhawks, and back in the Original Six days, when we played 14 games against every team every year, Gordie and I saw a lot of each other. As you can see, we're in a peaceful mood here. So peaceful that we've traded our No. 9 jerseys just for laughs.

HERE'S PIERRE PILOTE AGAIN WITH HIS WIFE ANN ON THE NIGHT THE BLACKHAWKS RETIRED THE NO. 3, which was also worn by Keith Magnuson—another favorite of mine—who tragically died in an auto accident. Pierre won the Norris Trophy three straight years and was a teammate on our 1961 Stanley Cup team. When I passed Pierre the puck, it wasn't to get an assist. It was to get the puck back in better position.

BOBBY AND PIERRE PILOTE SPENT **11 YEARS** AS BLACKHAWKS TEAMMATES.

THIS GROUP SHOT IS A MIXTURE OF YOUNG AND OLD. From left: Brent Seabrook, Jonathan Toews, Adam Burish, Patrick Kane, Tony O, myself, Stan Mikita, Duncan Keith, Patrick Sharp, and Denis Savard.

THE BLACKHAWKS PLAYED THE DETROIT RED WINGS IN THE NATIONAL HOCKEY LEAGUE'S WINTER CLASSIC ON NEW YEAR'S DAY 2009 AT WRIGLEY FIELD. As part of my job as ambassador, I helped to promote the game at the ballpark during the summer with Patrick Kane (center) and Jonathan Toews, who became captain of the Blackhawks at the unbelievable age of 21 and led the team to the 2010 Stanley Cup thanks to Kane's series-clinching goal. Those two kids remind me a little bit of when Stan and I were together on the 1961 champions. You'll note the "WWW" on their jerseys to honor the memory of Bill Wirtz, who died in 2007.

WHAT CAN I SAY ABOUT THIS PICTURE? It was before what the Blackhawks called "9/21 Night" on March 7, 2008, to welcome back golden oldies No. 9, yours truly, and No. 21, the great Stan Mikita. We were driven out on the United Center ice from the west end, where the Zamboni comes out, only our ride was a 1957 Chevrolet convertible. That was a muscle car from the same year I made it to the NHL. I don't know how they kept that automobile in such mint condition, but I imagine somewhere along the line, it needed some new parts. I know the feeling.

# MARCH 7, 2008
## THE NIGHT BOBBY AND STAN MIKITA WERE WELCOMED BACK TO THE UNITED CENTER AS BLACKHAWKS AMBASSADORS.

I GUESS THIS MADE IT OFFICIAL, when Stan and I stood for the national anthem along with John McDonough on the same 9/21 Night when we were announced as ambassadors for the Black-hawks. The singing of the anthem is always special at Blackhawks games, but this night really meant a lot to Stan and me. Stan played his whole career with the Blackhawks. I left when John was in college. A lot of time passed and I didn't think I'd ever been in a position like this again. I'm guessing Stan felt the same way.

THIS IS THE CEREMONIAL FACE-OFF ON 9/21 NIGHT before the Blackhawks played the San Jose Sharks. Jeremy Roenick, who came up to the NHL with the Blackhawks, is on the left. Jonathan Toews is on the right, wearing the "C" as was Stan Mikita. I had my "A" on from the time I was alternate captain. It was a short time, though.

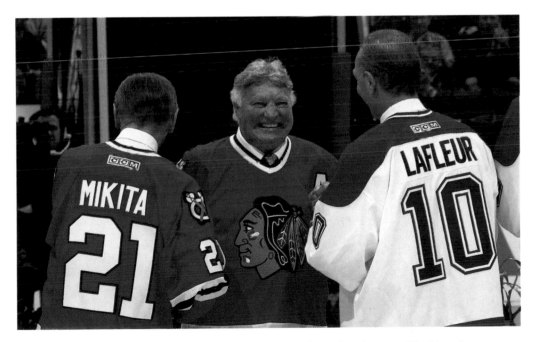

IN JANUARY OF 2009, the Canadiens invited a few of us former Blackhawks to Montreal for a pregame ceremony between the two teams to honor our Original Six rivalry. What a rivalry it was. Hall of Famer Guy Lafleur is with us. The Canadiens have always done everything with class, and that night was in keeping with their tradition.

FROM LEFT IN THE CUBS' TELEVISION BOOTH are Stan Mikita, Tony Esposito, and me. We have just finished singing during the seventh-inning stretch at Wrigley Field.

HERE I AM AT WRIGLEY FIELD AGAIN, with my No. 9 Chicago Cubs jersey. I played some baseball, you know, when I was young. Anyway, it's a tradition at Cubs home games to have people sing "Take Me Out to the Ballgame" during the seventh-inning stretch. Tony Esposito, Stan Mikita, and I were there in May 2008, and my fellow ambassador, Tony O, says I got ahead of the music. "You went too fast," he said. He might have been right. As I recall, I sang the last verse twice.

I'M BESIDE A TRUCK AT THE WINTER CLASSIC IN 2009, a terrific idea of the NHL's. There was an outdoor game in Edmonton and then Buffalo before the one in Chicago, which was a huge success. In 2010, they went to Fenway Park in Boston. The games are on national TV, and are great for the game of hockey.

I'M INSIDE THE TRUCK HERE, trying to keep warm, even though it wasn't brutally cold on New Year's Day of 2009. The big worry about these games is that it will snow—which it did in Buffalo—but we got lucky at Wrigley Field, even though snow had been in the forecast.

MY EARMUFFS AND I WERE ON THE ICE WITH CHRIS CHELIOS, a Detroit defenseman who once played for the Blackhawks, and "Terrible" Ted Lindsay, a Hall of Famer who also played with both franchises during his great career. They called him "Terrible" because he was a fierce competitor.

A CEREMONIAL FACE-OFF WITH BASEBALL AND HOCKEY PLAYERS. From left: Ferguson Jenkins, Denis Savard, Ryne Sandberg, myself, Ted Lindsay, Tony Esposito, Billy Williams, and Stan Mikita. The two actual players taking the face-off are Nicklas Lidstrom of the Red Wings and Hawks captain Jonathan Toews.

MY EARMUFFS AND I AGAIN, enjoying every minute of what was a terrific Winter Classic, even though the Red Wings beat the Blackhawks. My wife Deborah was responsible for the protective gear. I don't know that I would have chosen leopard skin, but it worked. This is how most of us learned how to play hockey. In the NHL, fans pile into nice warm arenas during the winter to watch games. But as kids in Canada, until we joined organized programs, we played on frozen ponds or lakes or wherever, with no roof over our heads.

# 40,818 ATTENDANCE AT WRIGLEY FIELD FOR THE 2009 NHL WINTER CLASSIC.

THIS IS PART OF A RED CARPET CEREMONY OUTSIDE THE UNITED CENTER, another way the new management made fans feel more a part of the Blackhawks. In my playing days, we tried to reach out to the public. But now, the organization does it all the time, and fans appreciate the effort.

HERE ARE THE FOUR AMBASSADORS—Savard, Mikita, Esposito, and myself—in the Blackhawks locker room. We're joined by Marian Hossa, who played in the Stanley Cup Finals for his third different team in 2010. After losing with Pittsburgh and Detroit, he finally got his ring in Chicago.

I TOLD YOU THIS NIGHT WAS ONE I WILL NEVER
FORGET, and just to make sure you don't forget it, here's another view of October 10, 2009. The Blackhawks had opened
their regular season with two games in Finland, and expecta-
tions were sky-high as the team opened its home schedule
before a packed United Center. Patrick Kane on the left and
Jonathan Toews on the far right are bookends to us ambassadors—Savard, Tony O, Mikita, and yours truly. I'm not sure
the young stars knew we were part of the program that night.
I know it was a surprise to the fans, not that management
needed us to sell tickets to watch this team.

# OCTOBER 10, 2009

THE DATE
OF THE
BLACKHAWKS'
HOME OPENER
AND A SPECIAL
APPEARANCE
BY BOBBY HULL.

I'M SMILING AND WAV-
ING TO THE CROWD
AS I SKATE ONTO THE
UNITED CENTER ICE, but
deep down, I was as nervous
as when I was playing back in
the day. The welcome by the
greatest fans in the world was
fabulous, but I was concerned
that I was not in complete
control of my reflexes. We had
held a "secret" practice the
day before. Tony O said he
felt great putting on the pads
again, and Savard, of course,
still skates like the wind. But
after being announced last of
the four, I wasn't sure how
this adventure was going
to end, if you know what I
mean. I'm glad there were
others there to look out for
me in case I blew a tire. I
needed them for brakes, that's
for sure.

THE STANLEY CUP AND
I WERE REUNITED during
the opening ceremony of the
2010 Blackhawks Convention
at the Hilton Chicago on July
30, 2010.

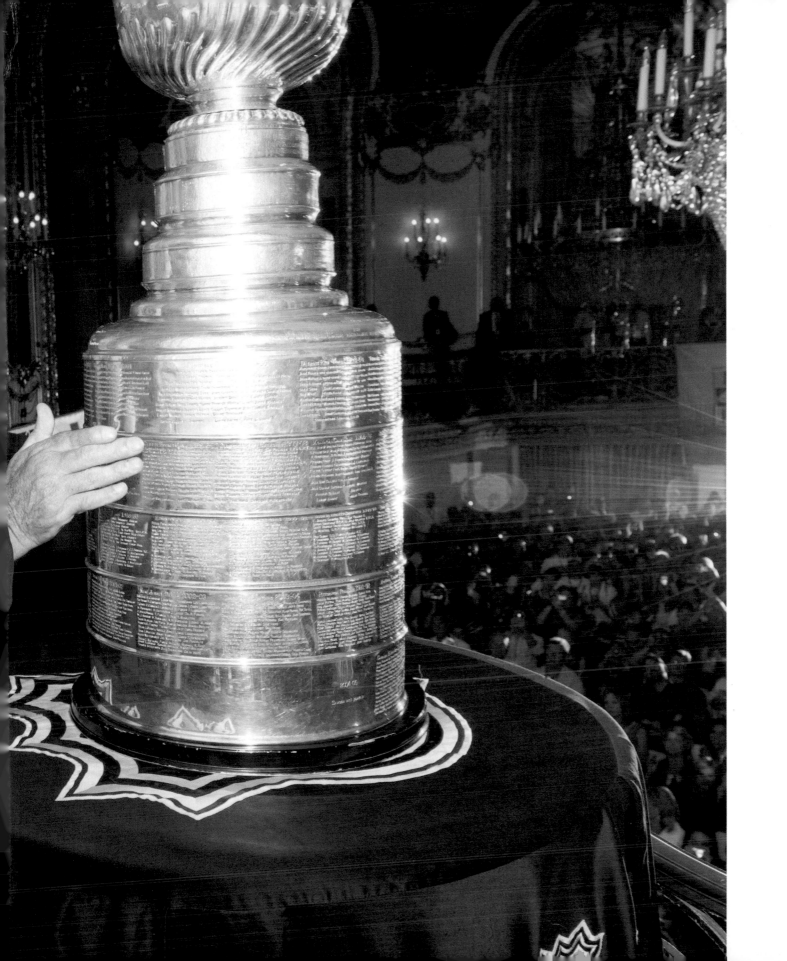

# Acknowledgments

THIS BOOK IS DEDICATED TO MY TWO FAVORITE GIRLS: my mother Lena and my wife Deborah. While my father was telling me I would never amount to a hill of beans, my mother was saying, "Robert, there isn't a mountain too high for you to scale, there isn't a river too wide for you to cross, and there isn't a prairie too vast for you to plow." After every game she watched me play, it felt like she skated more strides and took more shots than I had. She crossed her fingers, her arms, and her legs to bring me good luck—if she had been able to cross her eyes, she would have done that, too. In her eyes, no one was more talented than her Robert, and I took that knowledge with me into every game. She was proud of her No. 1 son and I was proud of her. If you wanted a fight, just say one bad word about Robert Marvin Hall—Lena would be ready to drop the gloves in an instant.

My wife Deborah never complains about the time I spend away from home as an ambassador for the wonderful Chicago Blackhawks family. While I attend to the most important people in our business—the hockey fans in the Chicagoland area and across North America—she has made our houses into homes with her deft touch as a decorator. Everywhere we have lived, her gardens have been the most beautiful on the block, and inside our homes nothing was ever overlooked. As Deborah always says, "A place for everything, and everything in its place."

My love and sincerest thanks to the two most important girls in my life for always being close when I needed it.

—Bobby Hull

AS A YOUNG REPORTER with the *Chicago Tribune*, I was assigned to write about the Blackhawks in the late 1960s. One of my early tasks was to interview Bobby Hull. After 10 minutes I was spoiled forever, because I assumed that every professional athlete would be as genial and honest. During the ensuing 40 or so years, I realized that the Golden Jet in particular, and hockey players in general, were different. Well, Bobby Hull still is, and it is my honor to be a small part of this book chronicling the career of one of the most gifted individuals—and finest ambassadors—in sports history. I also wish to thank the support of the Blackhawks organization, especially Rocky Wirtz, John McDonough, Jay Blunk, Pete Hassen, and Chase Agnello-Dean. They helped mightily in making this project happen, as did Adam Motin, Tom Bast, and Mitch Rogatz of Triumph Books, and Jim Pender, a close friend of Hull's who was invaluable in organizing the many snapshots of his legacy, on and off the ice. I am not sure what it means to possess a photographic memory, but I am quite sure that if such a thing exists, Pender has it. Show him a picture, and you are bound to elicit pertinent names, dates, and places.

—Bob Verdi